NEED to KNOW

Key facts at your fingertips

AQA A-LEVEL BUSINESS

Neil James

HODDER
EDUCATION
AN HACHETTE UK COMPANY

Hachette UK's policy is to use papers that are natural, renewable and recyclable products and made from wood grown in sustainable forests. The logging and manufacturing processes are expected to conform to the environmental regulations of the country of origin.

Orders: please contact Bookpoint Ltd, 130 Park Drive, Milton Park, Abingdon, Oxon OX14 4SE. Telephone: (44) 01235 827827. Fax: (44) 01235 400401. Email education@bookpoint.co.uk

Lines are open from 9 a.m. to 5 p.m., Monday to Saturday, with a 24-hour message answering service. You can also order through our website: www.hoddereducation.co.uk

ISBN: 978 1 5104 2850 8

First published in 2018 by

Hodder Education,
An Hachette UK Company
Carmelite House
50 Victoria Embankment
London EC4Y 0DZ

Impression number   10 9 8 7 6 5 4 3 2 1

Year   2022 2021 2020 2019 2018

Typeset in India by Aptara Inc.

Printed in Spain

A catalogue record for this title is available from the British Library.

MIX
Paper from
responsible sources
FSC™ C104740
www.fsc.org

Contents

1 What is business? 5

2 Managers, leadership and decision making 15

3 Decision making to improve marketing performance 23

4 Making marketing decisions: using the marketing mix 32

5 Decision making to improve operational performance 39

6 Decision making to improve financial performance 48

7 Decision making to improve human resource performance 59

8 Analysing the strategic position of a business 70

9 Choosing strategic direction 93

10 Strategic methods: how to pursue strategies 97

11 Managing strategic change 108

Getting the most from this book

This *Need to Know* guide is designed to help you throughout your course as a companion to your learning and a revision aid in the months or weeks leading up to the final exams.

The following features in each section will help you get the most from the book.

You need to know

Each topic begins with a list summarising what you 'need to know' in this topic for the exam.

Exam tip

Key knowledge you need to demonstrate in the exam, tips on exam technique, common misconceptions to avoid and important things to remember.

Key terms

Definitions of highlighted terms in the text to make sure you know the essential terminology for your subject.

Do you know?

Questions at the end of each topic to test you on some of its key points. Check your answers here: www.hoddereducation.co.uk/ needtoknow/answers

End of section questions

Questions at the end of each main section of the book to test your knowledge of the specification area covered. Check your answers here: www.hoddereducation.co.uk/needtoknow/answers

1 What is business?

1.1 The nature and purpose of business

You need to know

- why businesses exist
- the relationship between mission and objectives
- the measurement of profit
- the different forms of business and the reasons for choosing a particular form
- the role of shareholders, why they invest and influences on share price
- the effects of ownership on mission, objectives, decisions and performance
- how the external environment can affect costs and demands
- the effect of competition, market conditions, incomes, interest rates, demographic factors, environmental issues and fair trade

Why businesses exist

Businesses exist in many shapes and sizes and for different purposes. These purposes are illustrated in Figure 1.

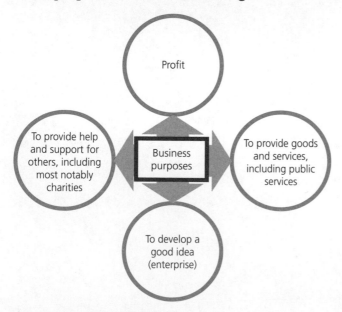

Figure 1 Business purposes

A business's **mission statement**:

■ is sometimes called the *vision statement*

■ tries to define what an organisation is, why it exists and its reason for being

The mission statement is a declaration of the business's core purpose and focus, for example NIKE Inc.'s is to 'Bring inspiration and innovation to every athlete in the world'.

The purpose of the mission statement is to bring focus and act as a guide when making critical decisions that may affect the direction of a business.

Common business objectives

When looking at the **objectives** of a business it is important to remember:

■ they may be complex

■ they will vary according to circumstances and the type of organisation

■ a charity will have different objectives to a public limited company

■ they may change over time

Three key objectives of business are:

■ survival   ■ growth   ■ profit

The global nature of business and competition in many markets has meant other objectives have taken on increasing importance, including:

■ customer service

■ corporate social responsibility (CSR)

Each functional area of a business will also set objectives that hopefully will contribute to the business achieving its overall objectives. This is illustrated in Figure 2.

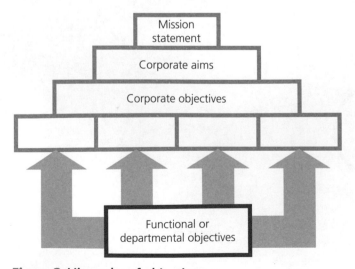

Figure 2 Hierarchy of objectives

Relationship between mission and objectives

The mission statement of a business outlines the bigger picture and perhaps establishes the core values and principles that help guide the conduct and actions of staff.

Objectives, however, are the goals that have been set to achieve the overall mission of the business.

Without the mission statement the objectives have no direction, but without the objectives the mission is unachievable. Together they provide a balance that helps shape a business's operation and service.

Objectives should be SMART:
- **s**pecific
- **m**easurable
- **a**chievable
- **r**ealistic
- **t**ime-based

Why businesses set objectives

Businesses set objectives:
- to evaluate performance
- to provide motivation for those who are responsible
- to give meaning to planning and ensure that a business remains focused on its mission

Measurement and importance of profit

Profit is the incentive for setting up a business or is the reward owners receive for taking the risk of investing in the business. Profit is calculated using the formula:

profit = total revenue – total cost

Revenue (also called *turnover*, *sales turnover* and *sales revenue*) is the money received from sales. Revenue is calculated using the formula:

revenue = units sold × sales price

Costs are divided into the following categories:
- **variable costs**
- **fixed costs**

Fixed costs plus variable costs represent the **total costs** of production in a given time period.

Key terms

Profit The amount of money remaining once all costs have been deducted from the revenue.

Revenue The money received from sales.

Variable costs Costs that vary directly with the level of output.

Fixed costs Costs that don't vary as a result of changes in the level of output.

Total costs Fixed costs plus variable costs.

1.2 Understanding different business forms

Private sector business

Businesses in the **private sector** fall into two broad categories, as shown in Table 1.

Table 1 Types of business

Corporate businesses	Non-corporate businesses
■ Private limited companies ■ Public limited companies	■ Sole traders (or sole proprietors) ■ Partnerships

Corporate businesses

The features of **corporate businesses** are:
- they have a legal identity separate from that of their owners
- owners benefit from **limited liability**

Shareholders' liability may be limited:
- by the value of the shares that each shareholder has purchased
- to the amount he or she has agreed to pay in the event of the business being wound up — more common with not-for-profit businesses

There are two main types of corporate company (see Table 2).

Table 2 The two main types of corporate company

Private limited companies	Public limited companies
■ Normally much smaller than public limited companies ■ Share capital must not exceed £50,000 ■ 'Ltd' must be included after the company's name ■ Often family businesses	■ Must have the term 'plc' after their name ■ Minimum capital of £50,000 ■ Have to publish more details of their financial affairs than do Ltd companies

Those forming a company must send two main documents to the Registrar of Companies:
- Memorandum of Association
- Articles of Association

Once these documents have been approved, the company receives a Certificate of Incorporation and can commence trading.

Non-corporate businesses

The features of non-corporate businesses are:
- the owners and their business are not treated as separate elements
- owners' private possessions are at risk in the event of failure
- sole traders and partners have unlimited liability

There are two main types of non-corporate business, sole traders and partnerships.

Sole traders (or proprietors) are:
- owned by a single person
- common in retailing and in services such as plumbing and hairdressing

Partnerships:
- comprise between two and twenty people
- are usually based on a Deed of Partnership
- some may include 'sleeping partners'
- are common in the professions, for example dentists and accountants

Other types of non-corporate business are not-for-profit businesses and mutuals.

Not-for-profit businesses' objectives might include:
- providing services to local communities
- giving people job-related skills
- fair-trading activities

Mutuals:
- are a form of business organisation
- are generally private businesses with an ownership base made up of clients and policyholders, for example insurance companies and some building societies

Many of the biggest building societies and insurance companies, however, have become plc's.

Public sector

Public sector organisations are services and businesses in the UK that are controlled and run by the government or local authorities, such as the police, fire service, BBC and NHS, as well as local council-run services such as rubbish collection.

As a result of **privatisation**, a number of key industries formerly in the public sector have been sold to the private sector, for example the steel, water and telephone industries.

Reasons for choosing different forms of business

The key choice is that between unincorporated and incorporated status. A number of factors may be considered:

- formalities and expenses — sole traders and partnerships are relatively easy to set up, with few formalities
- size and risk — if a business is, and intends to remain, small and carries little in the way of risk then a sole trader or partnership may be the most appropriate form
- the objectives of the owners — if the objectives of the owners involve growth then an incorporated business might be more appropriate as it may give greater access to capital and limited liability

Reasons for changing business form include:

- circumstances — due to the growth of a business, the owner(s) may wish to become incorporated in order to benefit from limited liability
- capital — the owner(s) of a business may find it easier to raise capital by becoming incorporated, or if it is a private limited by changing to public limited
- acquisition or takeover — this may cause a change of structure, for example a private limited may be taken over by a public limited

Role of shareholders and why they invest

Share capital is the money given to a company by **shareholders**:

- it is permanent and will never be paid back
- shareholders can get their money back by selling their shares through the stock market

Key terms

Public sector That part of the economy that is owned and controlled by the government or local authorities.

Privatisation The process of converting government-owned and -controlled industries and businesses to the private sector.

Shareholders The owners of a limited company, including any person, company or other institution that owns at least one share.

Exam tip

When deciding on the most appropriate legal structure for a business, always base any recommendation on the circumstances of the individual business, its objectives, size, product or service, and the risk involved.

Exam tip

We generally see businesses moving from Ltd to plc, but be aware that it is possible for a business to move from plc to Ltd, for example Richard Branson's Virgin.

■ any private individual can become a shareholder
■ the biggest shareholders are financial institutions, pension funds and insurance companies

Shareholders have certain rights and a role to play in the running of a business:

■ major decisions are required to be approved by the shareholders at a general meeting called by the directors
■ their main role therefore is to attend this meeting and discuss whatever is on the agenda, and to ensure the directors do not go beyond their powers
■ there are also certain things that can only be done by shareholders, such as removing the directors or changing the name of a company

There are two reasons why private individuals and financial institutions invest in shares:

■ income, known as a **dividend**
■ capital growth

Influences on share price and the significance of share price changes

The price of a share is determined by the market and the level of supply and demand. It is influenced by:

■ performance — better or worse than expected profits
■ expectation of better or worse profit performance
■ changes within the market or competitive environment
■ world uncertainty

The FT Small Cap Index tends to follow business confidence and economic cycle, as shown in Figure 3.

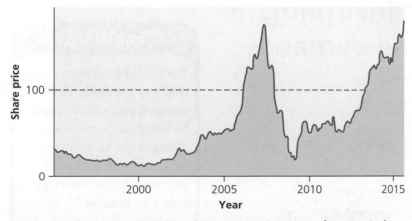

Figure 3 Chart showing how share price of Lookers (car dealer) coincides with consumer confidence (Source: Stockopedia)

Market capitalisation is calculated by the formula:

market capitalisation = share price × number of shares issued

- it gives a valuation of a company
- changes in the share price will affect the value of a business
- falling share price might provide an opportunity for investment or even takeover
- it might be an indication of a business in decline

The effects of ownership on mission, objectives, decisions and performance:

- profit is a key objective of many private sector businesses
- public limited companies are owned by shareholders and will often be driven by profit
- it may result in a very short-term approach to business decision making
- the philosophy outlined in the mission statement may therefore take a back seat
- sole traders and private limited companies will be less affected by the need to achieve profits

Key term

Market capitalisation
Calculated as follows: share price × number of shares issued.

External environment
All the factors outside the control of a business that may impact its operation.

Do you know?

1 What is the difference between corporate and non-corporate businesses?
2 What is meant by the 'public sector'?
3 How is market capitalisation calculated?

1.3 Businesses operate within an external environment

How the external environment can affect costs and demand

The **external environment** refers to factors that:

- are outside the control of the business
- are uncertain and unpredictable
- may impact on strategic goals and objectives

These factors include:

- competition
- market conditions
- economic factors
- interest rates
- demographic factors
- environmental issues

Exam tip

Don't always assume that any change in the external environment will be negative. Sometimes changes can be positive for a business, and what is negative for one business might be positive for another.

Competition

Almost all businesses operate within a competitive environment:

- the strategies adopted by competitor firms therefore have an impact on a business
- a competitor may come up with an innovative product or service
- there is likely to be competition on price, which in turn puts pressure on costs

Market conditions

The characteristics of a particular market that will impact on demand and costs include:

- size
- growth rate
- any barriers to entry
- seasonal factors
- amount and intensity of competiton

Economic factors

This covers a range of factors:

- the stage of the economic cycle
- interest rates
- inflation
- incomes
- exchange rates

Interest rates

Interest rates can have a big impact both on the demand for goods and services provided by a business, and on their cost:

- rising interest rates result in higher costs of borrowing for loans and mortgages
- rising interest rates may encourage greater saving
- as a result, demand is likely to be lower
- not all businesses will be affected adversely, however
- discount retailers (e.g. Lidl) and cheaper restaurants and takeaways may benefit
- rising interest rates may also result in rising business costs, especially for high-geared businesses
- investment decisions might also be postponed due to rising interest rates

The above list deals with rising interest rates — the opposite is likely to occur with falling rates.

> **Exam tip**
>
> Make sure you understand the difference between price and costs — price being what consumers pay for the finished product or service, while costs refer to the costs associated with producing a product or service.

> **Key term**
>
> **Interest rates** The cost of borrowing money.

> **Exam tip**
>
> Not all businesses will be affected in the same way — some may gain from rising interest rates.

Demographic factors

Demography is the study of human populations, including:

- age
- sex
- income
- occupation
- birth rates
- death rates
- level of public health
- immigration

These affect:

- the level of demand
- the nature of the goods and services bought
- the structure of the working population

It is therefore important for businesses to anticipate and recognise the demographic changes taking place.

Environmental issues such as fair trade

Table 3 shows environmental issues and impacts.

Table 3 Environmental issues and impacts

Issue	Resulting in	Leading to
Pollution	Government legislation	Increased cost
Global warming	Media attention	Damaged reputations
Exploitation	Media attention	<ul><li>Impact on sales</li><li>Focus on more sustainable development</li><li>Concern for fair trade</li></ul>

Key term

Fair trade Achieving better prices, decent working conditions and fair terms of trade for farmers and workers in developing countries.

Do you know?

1 What are the pressures on business of operating in a competitive environment?

2 What are the main economic influences on a business?

3 What is meant by 'demographic factors'?

Exam tips

- By focusing on environmental concerns a business may create a USP, enhance its reputation and generate greater sales.
- The external factors affecting a business can be easily recalled using the following acronym: PESTLE — political, economic, social, technological, legal and environmental factors.

End of section 1 questions

1 Explain the relationship between the mission statement and objectives.

2 How do the objectives of a not-for-profit business differ from those of a public limited company?

3 Explain why people invest in shares and the factors that might influence a purchasing decision.

4 Briefly explain the possible impact of rising interest rates on a car manufacturer.

5 Outline the potential benefits to a business of adopting good environmental policy.

2 Managers, leadership and decision making

2.1 Understanding management and leadership

You need to know

- the role of managers, the types and effectiveness of management styles and influences on them
- the value of scientific decision making, including the use and value of decision trees
- the influences on decision making
- stakeholder needs, including stakeholder mapping
- the overlap and potential conflict of interest between stakeholders
- the influences on the relationship between stakeholders and how to manage these relationships

What managers do

Figure 4 features a range of tasks managers do.

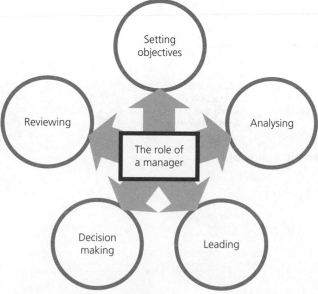

Figure 4 **Role of a manager**

Types of management and leadership styles

There are a number of different styles of leadership:

- autocratic — leader makes decisions without consulting others
- democratic — leader makes the final decision but includes others in the process
- laissez-faire — leader allows team members freedom in their work and in meeting deadlines
- paternalistic — leader consults and tries to make decisions in the best interest of all
- bureaucratic — leader does everything exactly by the rules

The Tannenbaum Schmidt continuum (see Figure 5):

- illustrates the range of leadership styles, from telling to delegating
- classifies the style according to how much a leader tells or listens to their staff
- shows that as workers' freedom in decision making increases, so the manager's authority decreases

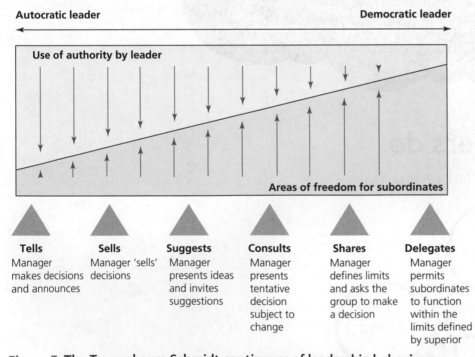

Figure 5 The Tannenbaum Schmidt continuum of leadership behaviour

The Blake and Mouton leadership grid (see Figure 6) portrays leadership through a grid, depicting:

- concern for people on the y-axis
- concern for production on the x-axis

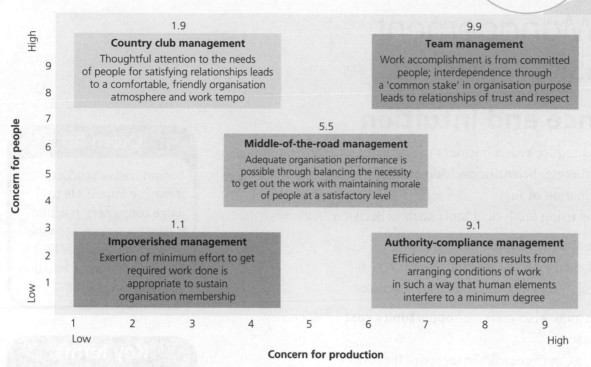

Figure 6 Blake and Mouton's leadership grid

The grid results in five leadership styles:

- country club — emphasis is on people, with little concern for task
- authority-compliance — emphasis is on task, with little concern for people
- impoverished — little concern for either task or people
- middle of the road — focus is on both task and people (a compromise)
- team leadership — high focus on both task and people

Effectiveness of different styles of leadership and management

The effectiveness and influences of the style of leadership may be affected by:

- the individual
- the nature of the industry
- the business culture
- circumstances
- the economic climate

Exam tip

It should not be assumed that there is one best style of leadership, as the style adopted is likely to depend on and evolve with the circumstances a business finds itself in.

Do you know?

1 What are the key aspects of a leader's role?

2 What are the key features of three different leadership styles?

2.2 Management decision making

Science and intuition

In order to reduce risk a business may adopt a scientific approach to decision making. **Scientific decision making** is based on:

- the collection of facts
- analysis using analytical tools such as decision trees

By contrast, with **intuition** decisions are:

- made based on a gut feeling
- not based on evidence or rational processes

Managers may also consider **opportunity cost** in decision making, as:

- resources, particularly finance, are limited
- they will not be able to undertake everything they would like to
- a choice has to be made

Use and value of decision trees

Decision trees are tree-like diagrams that can help when deciding between different options (see Figure 7). They create a visual representation of the various:

- risks
- rewards
- outcomes of each option

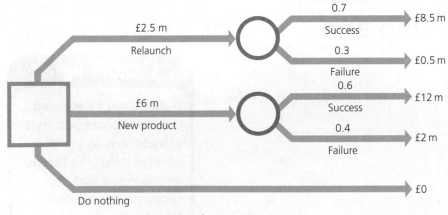

Figure 7 Decision tree for XYZ plc

By quantifying decisions, decision trees can reduce risk and help overcome uncertainty.

The key features of drawing and evaluating a decision tree:

■ every decision tree will begin with a square — this represents the decision to be made
■ from the square will come at least two lines, representing the possible options
■ there will often be a third line, the do-nothing option

Taking each line in turn, it is necessary to decide whether it is a result, is uncertain or whether another decision has to be made:

■ for a result there is no more to do
■ uncertain will be represented by a circle
■ a decision will be represented by another square

From each circle lines will be drawn showing the possible outcomes. In order to evaluate the decision tree all lines need to be fully labelled. This involves indicating the following information on the decision tree:

■ the cost of each option
■ the potential outcomes
■ the probabilities

Finally, it is necessary to calculate the expected values:

■ for each circle, the outcomes are multiplied with the probabilities and added together
■ the cost of that option is then subtracted
■ the options can then be compared to see which provides the highest return

Decision trees do have limitations:

■ managers may be influenced by their own bias toward a particular option
■ probabilities, while based on past experience, are likely to be just guesstimates

Influences on decision making

■ mission and objectives
■ resource constraints
■ external environment
■ competition
■ ethics

> ## Exam tip
>
> Although the AQA specification does not require you to construct decision trees, an ability to construct them will certainly aid your understanding.

> ## Exam tip
>
> In making a decision, a business is likely to consider the opportunity cost and will be limited by the resources available.

> ## Do you know?
>
> 1 How does scientific decision making differ from intuition?
> 2 What are the key influences on decision making?

2.3 The role and importance of stakeholders

Stakeholder needs in decision making

The various **stakeholders** and their interests are:

- employees — job security, good working conditions, pay
- customers — good customer service, value for money
- shareholders — capital growth, dividends
- suppliers — regular orders, on-time payment
- local communities — avoidance of pollution and congestion, employment
- government — employment, payment of taxes

Decisions taken by a business will have impacts on its various stakeholders and therefore it is important to consider and manage these stakeholder needs.

Stakeholder mapping is a technique for determining the importance of individual stakeholders. Mendelow drew up a matrix (see Figure 8) where stakeholders are categorised according to their:

- level of influence and power
- level of interest

> **Key term**
>
> **Stakeholder** Any individual or group with an interest in the activities and performance of a business.

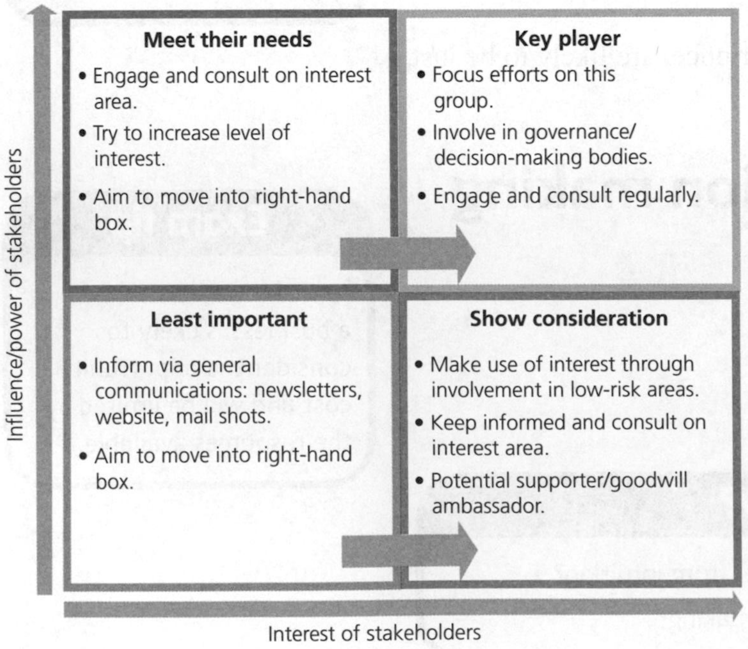

Meet their needs
- Engage and consult on interest area.
- Try to increase level of interest.
- Aim to move into right-hand box.

Key player
- Focus efforts on this group.
- Involve in governance/decision-making bodies.
- Engage and consult regularly.

Least important
- Inform via general communications: newsletters, website, mail shots.
- Aim to move into right-hand box.

Show consideration
- Make use of interest through involvement in low-risk areas.
- Keep informed and consult on interest area.
- Potential supporter/goodwill ambassador.

Influence/power of stakeholders

Interest of stakeholders

Figure 8 Mendelow's matrix

Management of stakeholders is then determined through the matrix according to whether:

- they are a key player
- their needs must be met
- consideration needs to be shown
- they are of least importance

Conflicting and overlapping needs

The potential overlap and conflict of stakeholder interests is illustrated in Table 4.

Table 4 The potential overlap and conflict of stakeholder interests

Decision	Overlap	Conflict
Relocate overseas	■ Shareholders: potential for lower costs and increased profit ■ Management: achieve objectives in terms of costs and profit	■ Local community: impact on local economy ■ Employees: lose jobs ■ Government: paid less tax
Introduce new technology	■ Shareholders and management: lower costs and potential profit ■ Consumer: may result in better quality and reliability	■ Employees: may lose jobs ■ Lower employment: could impact on local community
Expand production	■ Shareholders: higher sales and profit ■ Employees: job opportunities ■ Customers: greater availability ■ Suppliers: more orders ■ Government: more tax ■ Community: greater production	■ Local community: greater congestion and pollution
Increase price	■ Shareholders: potential profit increase ■ Management: improved performance ■ Government: more tax	■ Customers: cost more
Cut costs	■ Shareholders: potential profit ■ Management: achieve objectives	■ Employees: potential job loss ■ Customers: quality might be affected ■ Suppliers: pressure on prices
New markets/products	■ Shareholders: potential profit ■ Employees: job security ■ Suppliers: increased orders ■ Community: greater employment	■ Local community: pollution due to increased production

Influences on the relationship with stakeholders

Key features:
- power and interest
- leadership styles, for example whether autocratic or democratic

■ business objectives, for example some businesses may be committed to an ethical approach
■ government legislation, for example employment or environmental laws
■ state of economy — whether economy is booming or in recession

How to manage the relationship with stakeholders

There is always potential for conflict with stakeholders. This can be managed by:
■ stakeholder mapping
■ a culture of good communication
■ involvement and participation of stakeholders in decision making
■ careful planning

Exam tip

When evaluating the conflict of interest between stakeholder groups, a short-term vs long-term approach is often useful.

Do you know?

1 What is meant by the term 'stakeholder'?
2 Why is there a potential for conflict between stakeholders?

End of section 2 questions

1 How are leaders classified in the Tannenbaum Schmidt continuum?
2 What do you understand by decision trees and what are the benefits and drawbacks of these?
3 Identify four stakeholder groups, their interests and their potential conflicts.
4 How might Mendelow's matrix help in the management of stakeholders?

③ Decision making to improve marketing performance

You need to know

- marketing objectives: the value of setting them and the internal and external influences
- how to calculate market share, size, growth and growth in sales
- the value of primary and secondary research and sampling
- how to interpret marketing data, including correlation, confidence intervals and extrapolation
- the value of technology in gathering and analysing data
- the interpretation of price and income elasticity of demand and their value in marketing decisions
- the influences on and value of segmentation, targeting and positioning

Marketing is defined as 'the process responsible for identifying, anticipating and satisfying customer requirements profitably'.

3.1 Setting marketing objectives

Figure 9 shows the role of marketing in providing the link between a business and its customers.

Figure 9 Marketing: the link between the business and the customer

Marketing objectives might include:

- sales volume and sales value targets
- market and sales growth targets
- **market share** targets
- market size — knowing this enables realistic targets to be set

Key term

Market share The percentage of a market's total sales that is earned by a particular company over a specified time period.

Value of setting marketing objectives

The value of setting objectives might include:

■ target setting — gives focus and sense of direction
■ motivation — can be motivating for those responsible
■ evaluating performance — can be used to judge performance

Calculations for evaluating various marketing objectives are:

Market share	$\dfrac{\text{sales of firm}}{\text{total market sales}} \times 100$
Sales growth	$\dfrac{\text{difference in sales}}{\text{earliest year}} \times 100$
Market growth	$\dfrac{\text{difference in sales}}{\text{earliest year}} \times 100$
Market size	$\dfrac{\text{sales}}{\text{market share}} \times 100$

Exam tips

■ Students sometimes assume that just because sales are growing, market share automatically increases. This is not always the case, as in a growing market the sales of an individual business may be rising at a slower rate than others in the market.
■ The calculations you will be asked to perform in examinations are normally very straightforward provided you have learnt the formulae and undertaken regular practice of them.

Influences on marketing objectives and decisions

External and internal influences on marketing objectives and decisions are given in Table 5.

Table 5 External and internal influences on marketing objectives and decisions

External	Internal
■ Market and competition ■ Economic factors ■ Social factors ■ Ethics ■ Technology	■ Finance available ■ Production capacity ■ Human resources ■ Nature of product

Do you know?

1 What are the benefits of setting marketing objectives?
2 What is the difference between sales volume and sales value?

3.2 Understanding markets and customers

Value of primary and secondary market research

A business should fully understand the market it operates in. Market research helps by:

- studying market trends and characteristics
- establishing consumer profiles
- analysing market shares and potential of existing products
- forecasting sales for products
- analysing and forecasting sales of new products

Figure 10 shows the process of market research.

Primary and secondary research

Market research might be primary or secondary (Table 6).

Table 6

Primary research	Secondary research
- Also known as field research - Collects first-hand information - Answers specific issues or questions - Can be expensive	- Second-hand research - Uses data that already exist - Is cheap to collect - May not be directly related to the business

Sources of primary and secondary research are given in Table 7.

Table 7 Sources of primary and secondary research

Primary research	Secondary research
- Surveys/questionnaires - Observation - Focus groups - Test marketing	- Published reports - Government/agency data - Internet

Qualitative and quantitative research

Market research may also be separated into qualitative and quantitative research.

Key terms

Market research The process of gathering data on potential customers in order to reduce risk in decision making.

Primary research The collection of information for the first time for specific purposes.

Secondary research The collection of data that already exist and have been used for other purposes.

Figure 10 The process of market research

Qualitative market research:
- is designed to discover attitudes and opinions
- is collected from small groups known as focus groups
- may enable a business to design more appealing products

It can reveal consumer reactions to the:
- product
- pricing
- packaging

Quantitative market research:
- is the collection of data on consumer views
- can be statistically analysed
- can be represented in charts and graphs

Market mapping

Key features:
- enables a business to establish the position of its product(s) in the market
- reveals where most competition is
- may identify gaps in the market

In order to do this:
- two key features of a product or service are identified, for example price and quality
- a grid can then be established and the business or product(s) can be placed on the grid according to the quality (high or low) and price (high or low), as shown in Figure 11

> **Exam tip**
>
> It is not enough to know the various methods of market research. You need to be able to make some assessment of their value in particular circumstances.

> **Key terms**
>
> **Qualitative research** Research into the attitudes and opinions of consumers that influence their purchasing behaviour.
>
> **Quantitative research** The collection of information on consumer views and behaviour that can be analysed statistically.
>
> **Market mapping** A diagram that identifies all the products in the market using two key features, for example price and quality.

Figure 11 Market map of the UK supermarket industry

> **Exam tip**
>
> Do not assume that simply stopping every third person in the street will give a genuinely random sample. It will only give you a sample of people who are in the street at that time.

Value of sampling

Sampling is undertaken as:
- it is impossible to interview everyone
- it reduces the cost of research

There are a number of methods of sampling:
- random sampling
- stratified random sampling
- quota sampling

The larger the sample and the more information collected, the more reliable it should be — but the greater the cost to the firm will be. Factors that may influence choice of sampling include:
- budget available
- target market
- size of market and business

Interpretation of marketing data

Marketing data can be interpreted using various statistical tools, described below.

Correlation:
- occurs when there is a direct relationship between one factor and another, for example customer income and sales, or weather and sales (see Figure 12)
- may involve a positive or negative relationship
- enables more accurate forecasting

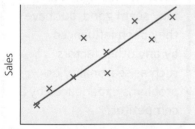

Figure 12 A positive correlation

Extrapolation:
- uses known data to predict future data — for example, by looking at past sales figures it may be possible to predict future sales
- is achieved by extending a **trend** line on a chart or graph
- needs to be treated with caution as it assumes the future will be similar to the past
- may not be suitable for industries subject to rapid change, for example fashion and technology

Confidence intervals:

- a business cannot be 100% certain of market research findings
- the confidence interval allows a margin of error
- an interval of 5% indicates that researchers are sure the results are correct +/–5%
- the interval used is likely to be affected by sample size — the bigger the sample, the lower the interval

Confidence level:

- this is an expression of how confident researchers are in the data collected
- it is expressed as a percentage
- the most commonly used confidence level is 95%

Technology and marketing decisions

Technology means that vast amounts of information can be collected, stored and analysed, as illustrated in Figure 13.

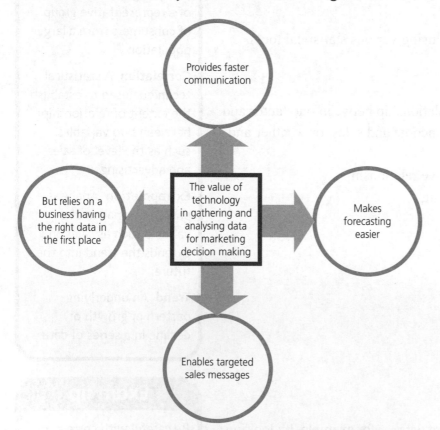

Figure 13 **The value of technology in gathering and analysing data for marketing decision making**

Price and income elasticity of demand data

Elasticity	percentage change in demand / percentage change in variable
Price elasticity of demand	% change in demand / % change in price
Income elasticity of demand	% change in demand / % change in income

An answer greater than 1 = elastic; less than 1 = inelastic (ignore minus signs).

Elasticity and marketing decisions

Price and income elasticity:

- can be used to evaluate the impact of changes in prices and incomes on sales
- might be volume or value
- will vary according to the type of product — luxury vs necessity

The likely effects of price changes are summed up in Table 8.

Table 8 **The likely effects of price changes**

	Price rise	Price fall
Elastic demand	Total revenue falls	Total revenue rises
Inelastic demand	Total revenue rises	Total revenue falls

Besides elasticity, other factors considered in decision making include:

- brand loyalty
- competitor actions
- consumer tastes and fashion
- availability of substitutes

Use of data in marketing decision making and planning

Data help reduce risk and uncertainty and create a better understanding of:

- the market
- the environment
- consumers

Key term

Elasticity A measure of the responsiveness of demand to a change in a variable, for example price or income.

Exam tip

When looking at a figure for elasticity, ignore the minus sign. If the answer is greater than 1 then demand is elastic; if it is less than 1 then it is inelastic.

Exam tip

Elasticity changes over time and it is important in decision making to use the most up-to-date figure. A figure even a year old may be out of date as the market may have changed or competitors may have introduced new products etc.

Do you know?

1 How does primary market research differ from secondary market research?

2 What is the value of sampling?

3 What is the difference between correlation and extrapolation?

3.3 Making marketing decisions: segmentation, targeting, positioning

Market segmentation may be by:

- age
- sex
- income etc.

Market targeting is when a business targets its marketing at a specific market segment (or target market).

Market positioning refers to how a consumer views an individual brand relative to other brands:

- price
- product
- services
- image

The objective is to have a brand that stands out in consumers' minds.

Segmentation, targeting and positioning are linked:

Segmentation → Targeting → Positioning

- segmentation breaks the market into clearly definable groups
- the group(s) to aim the product or service at will then be determined
- finally, the positioning of the product will be considered

The benefits and drawbacks of this process are given in Table 9.

Table 9 Benefits and drawbacks of this process

Benefits	Drawbacks
■ More effective marketing ■ Resources will be used more effectively ■ Sales and market share may increase	■ May overlook a potentially profitable segment ■ Changes in taste and fashion could be overlooked

Key terms

Market segmentation Dividing the market into identifiable sub-markets, each with its own customer characteristics.

Market targeting Deciding which segment a business wants to operate in.

Market positioning is where a particular brand stands in relation to other brands in the market.

Exam tip

There is a link between market positioning and market mapping. A business might use market mapping to determine the position of its product or service in the market.

Influences on choosing a target market and positioning

Influences include:

- the nature of the product
- competition
- the consumer

The benefits and drawbacks of niche marketing and mass marketing are given in Table 10.

Key terms

Niche marketing When businesses identify and satisfy the demands of small segments of a larger market.

Mass marketing When businesses aim their products at most of the available market.

Table 10 Niche vs mass marketing

	Niche marketing	Mass marketing
Benefits	■ May benefit from price skimming ■ Customer loyalty ■ Niche markets can be highly profitable	■ Produce on a large scale ■ Capital-intensive ■ Minimise unit costs
Drawbacks	■ May be difficult to generate sufficient profit ■ If profitable, could attract new competition	■ More competitive

Do you know?

1 Explain the link between segmentation, targeting and positioning.

2 What is the difference between niche and mass marketing?

End of section 3 questions

1 How is it possible for sales to increase but market share to fall?

2 Why would a business wish to achieve brand loyalty?

3 In market research, 60% of respondents preferred a particular washing powder brand. What does a 5% confidence interval tell analysts about this result?

4 A business has calculated the price elasticity of its product at −2.3. What would be the impact on revenue of a price increase?

5 Briefly outline why demand for a luxury product is likely to be income elastic.

6 Briefly outline the benefits and potential drawbacks of market targeting.

4 Making marketing decisions: using the marketing mix

You need to know

- the influences and effects of changes in the marketing mix
- product portfolio analysis, including the Boston matrix, product life cycle and value of new product development
- pricing decisions, including penetration and skimming
- the promotional mix, including branding
- distribution decisions, including multichannel distribution
- the importance of, and influences on, an integrated marketing mix
- the value of digital marketing and e-commerce

4.1 The elements of the marketing mix (7Ps)

The **marketing mix** (or 7Ps) is the combination of marketing elements, shown in Figure 14.

Key term

Marketing mix The main variables comprising a firm's marketing strategy.

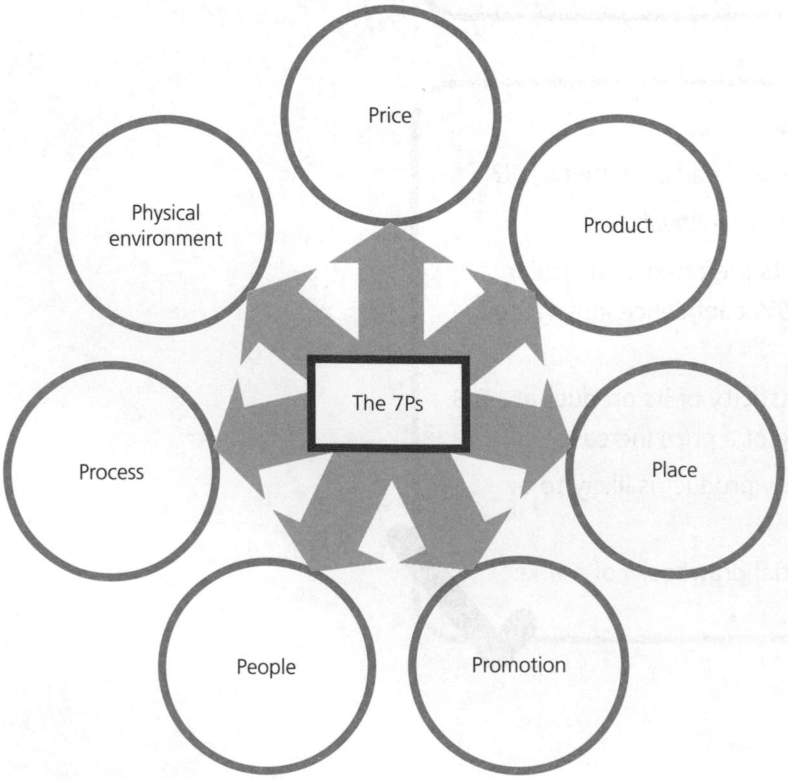

Price
Physical environment
Product
The 7Ps
Process
Place
People
Promotion

Figure 14 The 7Ps

Exam tip

When responding to questions about the marketing mix, do not write about all the elements as you are unlikely to have time to develop all points fully. Choose the most important two elements and write about those.

Influences on and effects of changes in the marketing mix

A range of factors will be considered in developing a marketing mix:

- finance
- the nature of the product
- technology
- market research

Product decisions

Factors influencing the development of new goods and services include:

- technology
- competitors' actions
- the entrepreneurial skills of managers and owners

A **unique selling point (USP)** is important and has a number of benefits:

- advertising campaigns can be based around the USP
- a USP assists in encouraging brand loyalty
- a USP may allow the firm to charge a premium price

In product portfolio analysis, the **product life cycle** is split into the stages shown in Figure 15.

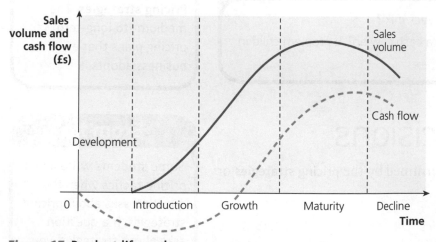

Figure 15 Product life cycle

The decline stage may be prolonged by implementing extension strategies, such as:

- finding new markets for existing products
- changing the appearance or packaging

Many businesses will have a range of products, known as the product mix or product portfolio. This can be analysed through the Boston matrix, which has four categories according to market share and market growth (see Figure 16):

■ star products
■ cash cows
■ dogs
■ problem children

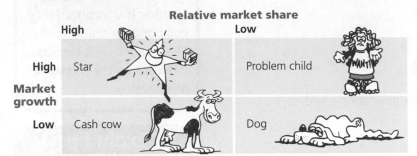

Figure 16 The Boston matrix

Possible decisions resulting from the Boston matrix:

■ cash cows can be milked for their revenue and profit
■ problem children need to be turned into rising stars
■ dogs might be discontinued
■ star products could become future cash cows
■ a business does not want too many products in a single category

Do you know?

1 What is meant by the term 'product mix'?
2 What is the difference between a cash cow and a problem child in the Boston matrix?

4.2 Pricing decisions

The **price of a product** may be determined by the **pricing strategies** or tactics adopted (see Table 11).

Table 11 Pricing strategies and tactics

Strategy	Tactic
■ Price skimming ■ Penetration pricing ■ Price leadership ■ Price taking	■ Loss leaders ■ Special-offer pricing ■ Psychological pricing

Key terms

Price of a product The amount that a business expects a customer to pay to purchase the good or service.

Pricing strategies The medium- to long-term pricing plans that a business adopts.

Exam tip

Some students write about pricing tactics when the question asks about pricing strategies. If a question asks about strategies, you must write about relevant pricing actions that a business can take in the long term, and not short-term tactical decisions.

Pricing decisions may be influenced by:
- costs
- marketing objectives
- elasticity of demand
- technology

Do you know?

1 What is the difference between a pricing strategy and a pricing tactic?
2 What are the three factors that may influence the pricing decision?

4.3 Decisions about the promotional mix

Promotion aims to:
- attract new customers and retain existing customers
- improve the position of the business in the market
- ensure the survival and growth of the business
- increase awareness of a product

The **promotional mix** refers to the range of methods used by businesses to communicate with customers, as shown in Figure 17.

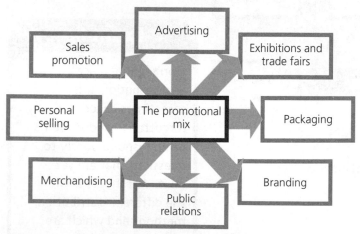

Figure 17 The promotional mix

The choice of promotional mix may be affected by:
- the product's position in the life cycle
- the type of product

Key terms

Promotion Bringing a product or business to consumers' attention.

Promotional mix The combination of methods used by businesses to communicate with prospective customers to inform them of their products and to persuade them to buy these products.

Exam tip

It is easy to think that promotion just means advertising. Good-quality answers to examination questions on this topic will demonstrate awareness of the circumstances in which each of the elements of the promotional mix might be appropriate.

Exam tip

Do not respond to questions about the promotional mix by writing about the marketing mix. Also, remember the promotional mix is more than just advertising.

- the finance available to the business
- where consumers make purchasing decisions
- competitors' actions

4.4 Distribution decisions (place)

The method of **distribution** chosen must fit with the rest of the product's marketing mix. It is influenced by:

- location
- credit terms
- willingness to display products in prominent positions

Three main distribution channels are shown in Figure 18.

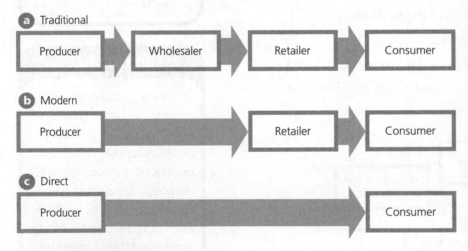

Figure 18 Channels of distribution

The choice of a distribution channel will be influenced by:
- the type of product
- the nature of the market
- the technical complexity of the product

Changing consumer trends mean many businesses now offer **multichannel distribution**.

Decisions relating to other elements of the marketing mix

People are the face of a business and can make or break a reputation. They need to be:

- helpful and polite
- motivated
- well trained

Process relates to the whole process of buying a product or service:

- from first entering a business premises or website
- to the delivery of the product or service
- and the after-sales service offered

The premises of a business (physical environment) should reflect the nature of the product.

An integrated marketing mix

An integrated marketing mix is one that:

- fits together
- addresses the elements of the mix
- portrays the correct image to consumers

There are a number of influences on an integrated marketing mix, as shown in Figure 19.

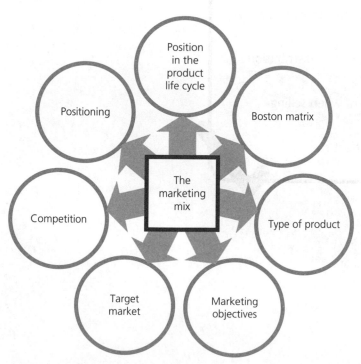

Figure 19 The marketing mix

The value of digital marketing and e-commerce

Benefits include:

- more detailed information available about consumers
- relationships more easily built with consumers
- greater contact between consumer and businesses
- social media have become very important
- can sell anywhere in the world

Do you know?

1 What is meant by 'multichannel distribution'?

2 How is the final 'P' of physical environment related to the marketing mix?

3 Briefly explain how digital marketing has benefited business.

End of section 4 questions

1 Briefly explain two factors a marketing manager will take into consideration when designing a marketing mix.

2 What do you understand by the product life cycle and the Boston matrix, and how might they be used in decision making?

3 Briefly explain two influences on the promotional mix of a newly opened restaurant.

4 Identify three factors that may affect the choice of distribution channel.

5 Why are people and process just as important when selling products as they are for selling services?

6 How do positioning and product life cycle affect the marketing mix?

5 Decision making to improve operational performance

You need to know

- the value of operational objectives and internal and external influences
- the calculation of operational data and their use in decision making and planning
- the importance of capacity, efficiency and labour productivity
- using technology in operations and how it may improve operational efficiency
- the benefits and difficulties of lean production
- how to choose the optimal mix of resources and how to use capacity effectively
- the importance of quality and methods of improvement
- the consequences of poor quality
- amount of inventory held, and value of improving flexibility, dependability and speed of response
- the influences on choice of suppliers, plus managing supply to match demand
- the value of outsourcing

5.1 Setting operational objectives

The operations function is responsible for:
- the actual production of goods or services
- turning inputs into outputs
- adding value

Value of setting operational objectives

Operational objectives must fit with corporate objectives and are likely to revolve around:
- costs of production
- quality of production
- speed of response and flexibility
- dependability
- environmental objectives

External and internal influences on operational objectives

External and internal influences on operational objectives are shown in Table 12.

Table 12 External and internal influences on operational objectives

External	Internal
■ Political and legal ■ Economic ■ Technological ■ Competition	■ Finance ■ Marketing ■ Human resources

Do you know?

1 What is meant by 'added value'?
2 List four operational objectives.

5.2 Analysing operational performance

Interpretation of operations data

Operations data include four main areas for which targets may be set:
■ capacity
■ capacity utilisation
■ productivity
■ unit costs

Calculation of operations data

Capacity is the total or maximum amount a business can produce in a given time.

Capacity utilisation	$\dfrac{\text{actual output in time period}}{\text{maximum possible output per period}} \times 100$
Labour productivity	$\dfrac{\text{output per time period}}{\text{number of employees}}$
Unit cost	$\dfrac{\text{total cost}}{\text{units of output}}$

Use of data in operational decision making and planning

There are a number of relationships to note:

- the productivity of a workforce increases with increased capacity utilisation
- unit costs decline with increased capacity utilisation
- changing the number employed will impact on productivity levels

Do you know?

1 What is the difference between capacity and capacity utilisation?
2 Describe how to calculate capacity utilisation, labour productivity and unit cost.

5.3 Increasing efficiency and productivity

How to choose the optimal mix of resources

Operational efficiency is all about getting more output from a given level of resources — the factors of production (see Figure 20).

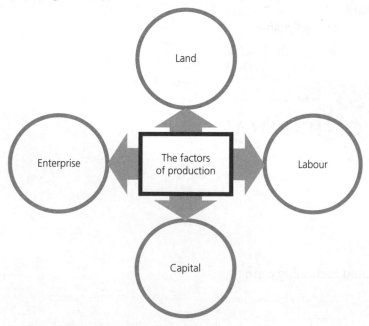

Figure 20 Factors of production

A business might adopt a **capital-intensive** or **labour-intensive** approach. The approach adopted depends on:

- the nature of the business
- the nature of the product
- the location

Importance of capacity

Capacity is the total that can be produced.

Capacity utilisation is the percentage of total capacity being produced.

Excess capacity is the difference between total capacity and the actual amount produced.

The higher the capacity utilisation, the lower the unit costs, but some excess capacity is useful as it:

- gives some flexibility
- provides scope for new orders
- could be important in a growing market
- provides scope for proper maintenance

Using capacity efficiently

A business will aim for an optimum level of capacity. Possible responses to excess or lack of capacity are given in Table 13.

Table 13 **Responses to excess or lack of capacity**

Excess capacity	Lack of capacity
■ Increase sales ■ Reduce capacity ■ Find alternative uses for plant	■ Outsource ■ Increase capacity ■ Reduce demand, e.g. by dynamic pricing

How to use technology to improve operational efficiency

Types of technology used in operations include:

- advanced computer systems
- the internet
- computer-aided manufacture (CAM)
- computer-aided design (CAD)

The benefits and drawbacks of new and updated technology are shown in Table 14.

Table 14 Benefits and drawbacks of new and updated technology

Benefits	Drawbacks
■ Reduced unit cost ■ Greater competitiveness ■ Opportunities for premium pricing ■ Improved quality ■ Small to medium-sized businesses may benefit ■ Possible access to new markets ■ Reduced waste	■ Cost ■ Resistance to change ■ Possible training and recruitment

Labour productivity and how to increase it

Labour productivity might be improved by:
■ investment in technology
■ training and motivation
■ job redesign
■ reducing the labour force

Difficulties of increasing labour productivity and efficiency

Difficulties include:
■ cost
■ quality
■ resistance of employees

Benefits and difficulties of lean production

Lean production is all about getting more from less. A key feature is the **just-in-time (JIT)** inventory (stock) strategy, which has the benefits and drawbacks shown in Table 15.

Table 15 Benefits and drawbacks of the just-in-time inventory strategy

Benefits	Drawbacks
■ Reduces waste ■ Reduces costs ■ Reduces space needed ■ May increase flexibility ■ Provides for greater motivation	■ Risks running out of stock ■ Loss of opportunities for bulk purchase ■ Requires trust in supplier

> **Exam tip**
>
> When considering improvements in productivity it is important to recognise that these should come without any reduction in quality or dependability of service.

> **Exam tip**
>
> Adopting a long-term vs short-term approach provides a good way of evaluating the worth of investing in improving labour productivity.

> **Key term**
>
> JIT An inventory strategy that companies employ to increase efficiency and decrease waste by receiving goods only as they are needed for production.

> **Exam tip**
>
> Although it is possible that bulk purchases may be lost, this may not be the case if during the course of a year the same volume of supplies is purchased. It is also possible that the supplier will save costs by producing JIT.

5.4 Improving quality
Methods of improving quality

Quality can be improved by:
- quality assurance
- total quality management (TQM)
- kaizen

Benefits and difficulties of improving quality

The benefits and difficulties of improving quality are shown in Table 16.

Table 16 Benefits and difficulties of improving quality

Benefits	Difficulties
■ Enhanced reputation and increased brand loyalty ■ Competitive advantage — quality may give a USP ■ Increased revenue due to higher sales ■ Greater flexibility in terms of price	■ Costs involved ■ Resistance to change

Consequences of poor quality

The consequences of poor quality revolve around increased costs:
- the cost of scrapping or reworking products
- the additional costs if goods are returned for repair or replacement
- the costs resulting from the damage to the business's reputation

Do you know?

1 Why is quality important to a business?
2 What is meant by 'TQM' and 'kaizen'?

Key terms

Quality assurance A system for ensuring the desired level of quality in the development, production and delivery of products or services.

Total quality management (TQM) A culture of quality throughout the organisation.

Kaizen The Japanese business philosophy of continuous improvement, where all employees are encouraged to identify and suggest possible improvements in the production process.

Exam tips

■ Implementing a system of TQM has enormous implications for the management of the workforce. It is likely to result in recruitment and training, and can have a positive effect on motivation. Seek to explore these links when responding to high-mark examination questions in this area.
■ Only quality assurance is mentioned in the specification, and although some textbooks will cover quality control it is important the two are not confused.

5.5 Managing inventory and supply chains

Inventory is the term used to describe stock, whereas the supply chain encompasses the whole process of providing a good or service for the consumer.

Flexibility, speed of response and dependability

Flexibility is the ability to meet a customer's requirements in terms of:

- numbers ordered
- variations in specification, for example by mass customisation

Speed of response is how quickly a business fulfils an order.

Dependability is its punctuality, or whether it fulfils the order on time.

Managing supply and demand

It is important that a business is able to match supply and demand.

Methods of managing demand	Methods of managing supply
- Additional marketing - Price changes - Sales promotions	- Flexible workforce - Increase capacity - Produce to order - Outsourcing

Value of outsourcing

The value of outsourcing and the dependencies of transferring production to a third party are shown in Table 17.

Table 17 **The value of outsourcing**

Value of outsourcing	Depends on
- Flexibility - Reliability - Possible lower costs	- Quality - Dependability - Relationship established with outsourced company

Key terms

Inventory Refers to the stock a business holds in the form of raw materials, components and work in progress.

Supply chain Involves the whole process of getting a good (or service) to the consumer.

Mass customisation The production of custom-tailored goods or services to meet customers' diverse and changing needs.

Outsourcing The transferring of production that was previously done in-house to a third party, in order to free up cash, time, personnel and facilities to concentrate on areas where the organisation has a competitive advantage.

Exam tip

Dependability can be used in the way described here, but it can also be used in terms of reliability and durability. It is important the correct context is identified when writing an answer.

Influences on the amount of inventory held

The level of inventory held depends on:
- the nature of the product
- the nature of production
- the nature of demand
- opportunity cost

An inventory control chart such as the one in Figure 21 might be used.

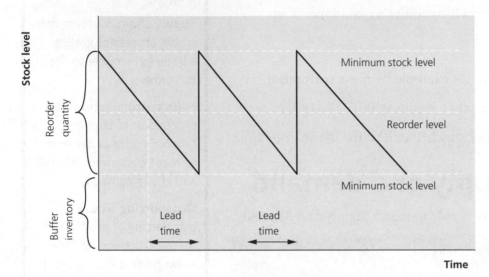

Figure 21 Inventory control chart

The key features of this chart are:
- buffer inventory
- reorder level
- lead time
- maximum stock level
- reorder quantity

Influences on the choice of supplier

Factors influencing the choice of supplier are:
- dependability
- flexibility
- quality
- price and payment terms
- ethics

Managing supply

Managing the supply chain is about having the right good in the right place at the right time. This requires:

- good communication with suppliers
- coordination with other functional areas
- an understanding of the external environment

Do you know?

1 What are the benefits of mass customisation?
2 What is meant by the term 'outsourcing'?
3 What are the factors that affect the level of inventory held?

End of section 5 questions

1 How may the functional areas of marketing and finance influence operational decision making?

2 Why do the unit costs of production decline when capacity utilisation and labour productivity increase?

3 How can labour productivity be improved and what are the benefits of doing so?

4 Why is poor quality likely to result in increased costs for a business?

5 In what circumstances might payment terms be more important than flexibility when choosing a supplier?

6 How may new technology impact the operations function?

⑥ Decision making to improve financial performance

You need to know

- the value of setting financial objectives and the internal and external influences on them
- the distinction between cash flow and profit, and between gross profit, operating profit and profit for the year
- the objectives concerning revenue, costs and profit, cash flow, capital expenditure and capital structure
- the value of and how to construct and analyse budgets, cash flow forecasts and break-even charts
- how to analyse profitability and the timings of cash inflows and outflows
- the use of data for financial decision making and planning
- the various internal and external sources of finance and their benefits and drawbacks
- the methods and difficulties of improving cash flow profits and profitability

6.1 Setting financial objectives

The benefits of setting financial objectives are:

- as a measure of performance
- as targets that can be a focus for decision making
- that potential investors or creditors may be able to assess the viability of the business

Objectives for investment (capital expenditure) levels

Capital expenditure objectives may depend on:

- the overall corporate objectives
- the type of business
- the state of the economy and the market the company operates in

Return on an investment is a possible objective, for example 10%. This percentage is calculated using the formula:

$$\frac{\text{return from investment (or profit)}}{\text{capital invested}} \times 100$$

This calculation might also be used when deciding between two different investments.

> ### Key term
>
> **Capital expenditure**
> Money used to purchase, upgrade or improve the life of long-term assets.

Capital structure objectives

Capital structure refers to the long-term capital (finance) of a business, made up of **equity** and **borrowing**.

The proportion of borrowing to equity is important as:
- the higher the borrowing, the greater the interest repayment
- high interest payments could put a business at risk if profit should fall
- any rise in interest rates could have a big impact on profit

Targets may be set in terms of the proportion of long-term capital that is debt. This is measured by the gearing ratio, which is calculated using the formula:

$$\frac{\text{loan capital}}{\text{total capital}} \times 100$$

where total capital = loan capital + equity.

Key terms

Equity The money that a business raises through the issue of shares.

Borrowing The money that a business raises through loan capital.

Revenue, costs and profit objectives

Revenue provides the starting point for a budget. Objectives for revenue might depend on:
- the type of market a business is operating in
- the state of the economy

These would need to be coordinated with the other functional areas.

The competitive environment necessitates cost and profit objectives, such as shown in Table 18.

Table 18 Cost and profit objectives

Cost objectives	Profit objectives
■ Unit cost targets ■ Specific targets for individual costs ■ Overall cost minimisation	■ A particular figure ■ A percentage increase ■ In terms of profit margin

Exam tip

Profit maximisation is sometimes identified as an objective but it is difficult to judge whether this has been achieved, and a business making unreasonably high profit can be the subject of a great deal of criticism.

Gross profit, operating profit and profit for the year

Gross profit is calculated using the formula:

gross profit = sales revenue – direct costs of production

Operating profit is calculated using one of two formulae:

operating profit = sales revenue – all costs of production

or:

operating profit = gross profit – expenses

Key terms

Gross profit The difference between a business's sales revenue and the direct costs of production.

Operating profit The difference between the gross profit and the indirect costs of production.

Profit for the year is calculated using the formula:

$$\text{profit for the year} = \text{operating profit} + \text{other income} - \text{other expenditure}$$

Profit figures are most easily analysed by converting them to ratios or **profit margins** as follows:

Gross profit margin	$\dfrac{\text{gross profit}}{\text{sales revenue}} \times 100$
Operating profit margin	$\dfrac{\text{operating profit}}{\text{sales revenue}} \times 100$
Profit for the year margin	$\dfrac{\text{profit for the year}}{\text{sales revenue}} \times 100$

Once calculated, performance can then be assessed by:
- comparing figures to those of previous years
- comparing figures to those of similar businesses

Cash flow objectives

Cash flow objectives may vary according to circumstances and include:
- targets for monthly closing balances
- reduction of bank borrowings to a target level
- reduction of seasonality in sales
- targets for achieving payment from customers
- extension of the business's credit period to pay suppliers

Distinction between cash flow and profit

Cash flow is the difference between the actual amount of money a business receives (inflows) and the actual amount it pays out (outflows).

Profit is the difference between all sales revenue (even if payment has not yet been received) and expenditure.

A profitable business may have cash flow problems due to:
- holding large amounts of inventory (stock)
- having sales on long credit periods
- the purchase of fixed assets using cash

Influences on financial objectives and decisions

Table 19 shows the external and internal influences on financial objectives and decisions.

Table 19 External and internal influences on financial objectives and decisions

External influences	Internal influences
■ Competitor actions ■ Market forces ■ Economic factors ■ Political factors ■ Technology	■ Corporate objectives ■ Resources available ■ Operational factors

Do you know?

1 What is the value of setting financial objectives?

2 What is the difference between cash flow and profit?

3 How would you calculate return on investment, gross profit margin and net profit margin?

6.2 Analysing financial performance

Budgets and cash flow forecasts

A budget provides:

■ a target for entrepreneurs and managers

■ a basis for a later assessment of the performance of a business

Budgets are likely to be constructed for income and expenditure.

The process of constructing a budget is shown in Figure 22.

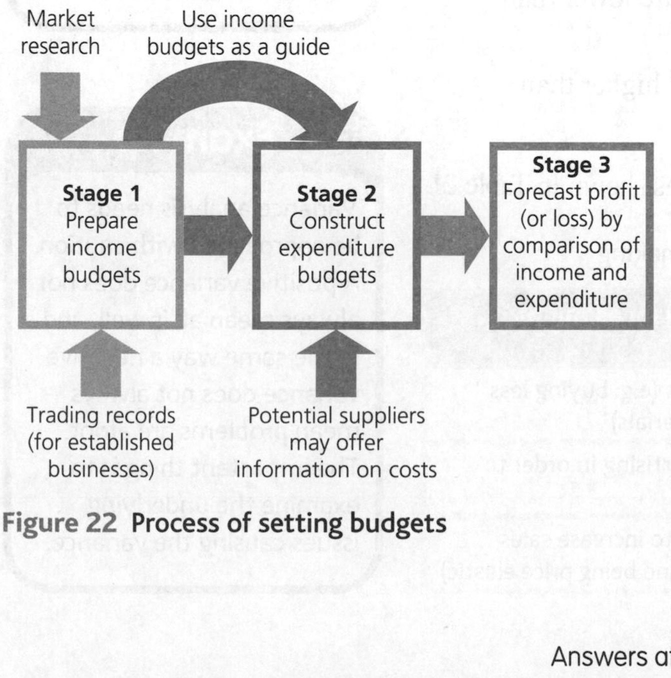

Figure 22 Process of setting budgets

> **Key term**
>
> **Budget** A financial plan.

Businesses set budgets because:
- they are an essential element of a business plan
- budgets can help businesses decide whether or not to go ahead with a business idea
- budgets can help with pricing decisions

The difficulties of setting budgets include:
- lack of data upon which to base a budget
- forecasting costs can be problematic
- competitors' actions may negate data used for budgeting

Value of budgeting

Budgets

The benefits and drawbacks of using budgets are given in Table 20.

Table 20 Benefits and drawbacks of using budgets

Benefits	Drawbacks
- Targets can be set for each part of a business - Inefficiency and waste can be identified - May focus decision making on the achievement of objectives - Should improve financial control by preventing overspending - May help improve internal communication - May be motivating for user while enabling managers to monitor and control	- Operation can become inflexible - Dependent on accuracy of data

Variance analysis

Variance analysis allows managers to examine the differences between planned activities in the form of budgets and the actual results achieved. The result may be:
- a positive (or favourable) variance when costs are lower than forecast or profit or revenues higher
- a negative (or adverse) variance when costs are higher than expected or revenues are less than anticipated

Variances can be used to inform decision making, as shown in Table 21.

Table 21 How to use variances to inform decision making

Positive variances might lead to:	Negative variances might lead to:
increased production if prices are rising	cost reductions (e.g. buying less expensive materials)
reduced prices if costs are below expectations and the aim is sales growth	increased advertising in order to increase sales
reinvestment in the business or higher dividend payments	reduced prices to increase sales (relies on demand being price elastic)

> **Exam tip**
>
> Remember that financial information given in the examination paper is often a forecast. It may not be accurate. You should treat this with caution, especially if you think that the quality of market research was poor.

> **Exam tip**
>
> When answering questions on the value of budgets, students often write only about the use of budgets in preventing overspending. Make sure that you can argue a wider range of points.

> **Key term**
>
> Variance analysis The study by managers of the differences between planned activities in the form of budgets and the actual results achieved.

> **Exam tip**
>
> Variance analysis needs to be approached with caution. A positive variance does not always mean all is well, and in the same way a negative variance does not always mean problems are afoot. The important thing is to examine the underlying issues causing the variance.

Cash flow forecasts

Cash flow forecasts comprise three sections:
- receipts
- payments
- running balance

How to analyse the timings of cash inflows and outflows

The analysis of the relationship between **payables** (money leaving) and **receivables** (money coming in) is important as it will enable a business to:
- forecast when cash outflows might exceed cash inflows
- plan when and how to finance major items of expenditure
- highlight any periods when cash surpluses may exist
- assess whether an idea will generate enough cash to be able to survive
- use the analysis as evidence when requesting a loan

How to construct and interpret break-even charts

A break-even chart is a graph used in break-even analysis to illustrate the point at which total costs are equal to total revenue.

A break-even chart is constructed as follows (see Figure 23):
- give the chart a title
- label the axes (horizontal — output in units; vertical — costs/revenues in pounds)
- draw on the fixed cost line
- draw on the variable cost line
- draw on the total cost line
- draw on the sales revenue line
- label the break-even point where sales revenue = total cost
- mark on forecast level of the company's output (SOP is selected operating output)
- mark on the margin of safety
- mark clearly the amount of profit and loss

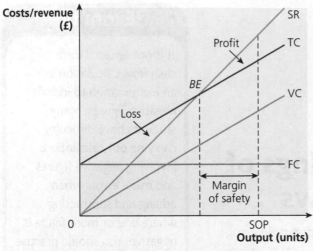

Figure 23 A break-even chart for product X

Contribution	sales revenue – variable costs
	or unit contribution × output
Unit contribution	sales price per unit – variable cost per unit
Break-even	$\dfrac{\text{fixed costs}}{\text{contribution per unit}}$
Profit	contribution total – fixed costs

> **Key term**
>
> **Contribution** The amount of money left over after variable costs have been subtracted from revenue.

The effects of changes in price, output and cost

The effects of changes in key variables on the break-even chart are illustrated in Table 22.

Table 22 Effects of changes in key variables on the break-even chart

Change in key variable	Impact on break-even chart	Effect on break-even output
Increase in selling price	Revenue line pivots upwards	Lower break-even output
Fall in selling price	Revenue line pivots downwards	Higher break-even output
Rise in fixed costs	Parallel upward shift in fixed and total cost lines	Higher level of output required to break even
Fall in fixed costs	Parallel downward shift in fixed and total cost lines	Lower level of output required to break even
Rise in variable costs	Total cost line pivots upwards	Higher level of output needed to break even
Fall in variable costs	Total cost line pivots downwards	Lower level of output needed to break even

> **Exam tip**
>
> When adding or amending lines on break-even charts, do not waste time by plotting figures at each level of output before drawing the new line. All lines on break-even charts are straight so it is only necessary to plot the new figures at zero and maximum output and to join up these two points using a ruler.

Value of break-even analysis

The benefits and drawbacks of break-even analysis are given in Table 23.

Table 23 Value of break-even analysis

Benefits	Drawbacks
■ Quick and easy to perform ■ Useful for new business start-ups ■ To support loan applications ■ To measure profits and losses ■ To model 'what if?' scenarios	■ No costs are truly fixed ■ The analysis is only as good as the information provided ■ Sales revenue assumes all output is sold and at a uniform price ■ The total cost ignores any bulk-buying discounts

Exam tip

It is common for examination questions to ask you to read data from break-even charts. You may be required to read off profit or loss, revenue or variable costs. You should practise doing this.

Use of data for financial decision making and planning

The use of data for financial decision making and planning is illustrated in Figure 24.

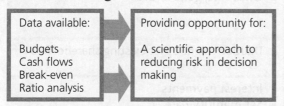

Figure 24 Use of data for financial decision making and planning

Do you know?

1 Why do businesses construct budgets?
2 What is meant by 'variance analysis'?
3 Explain the difference between payables and receivables.
4 Explain the weaknesses of break-even.

6.3 Making financial decisions: sources of finance

Internal and external sources of finance

Sources of finance can be internal or external, as shown in Table 24.

Table 24 Internal and external sources of finance

External (long-term)	Internal (long-term)
■ Equity ■ Loans ■ Venture capital ■ Mortgages ■ Crowdfunding	■ Retained profit ■ Sale of assets

There are also three external short-term sources available:

- overdraft
- debt factoring
- trade credit

Advantages and disadvantages of different sources of finance

Table 25 summarises the various sources of finance available to a business for short-term and long-term uses.

Table 25 Sources of finance available to a business

Source	Advantages	Disadvantages
Retained profit	■ No interest to pay ■ Does not have to be paid back ■ No dilution of shares	■ Shareholders may have reduced dividends
Sale of assets	■ No interest to pay ■ Does not have to be paid back ■ No dilution of shares	■ Once sold, gone forever
Equity	■ No interest to pay ■ Does not have to be paid back	■ Dilution might upset existing shareholders
Loans	■ No dilution of shares	■ Interest payments ■ Set maturity date
Overdraft	■ Quick and easy to set up and very flexible ■ Interest paid only on amount overdrawn	■ Interest payments higher than for a loan
Debt factoring	■ Immediate cash ■ Improves cash flow ■ Protection from bad debts ■ Reduced administration costs	■ Expensive ■ Customer relations may be affected
Trade credit	■ Eases cash flow ■ Buy now, pay later	■ If late paying, can damage credit history

Do you know?

1 What are the benefits of internal sources of finance?

2 What is meant by 'debt factoring'?

6.4 Making financial decisions: improving cash flow and profits

Methods of improving cash flow

Causes of cash flow problems and methods of improving cash flow are given in Table 26.

Table 26 Causes of cash flow problems and methods of improving cash flow

Causes of cash flow problems	Methods of improving cash flow
■ Poor management ■ Giving too much trade credit ■ Overtrading ■ Unexpected expenditure	■ Debt factoring ■ Sale and leaseback ■ Improved working capital control

Control of **working capital** can help cash flow management by:
■ selling stocks of finished goods quickly
■ making customers pay on time and offering less trade credit
■ slowing cash outflows
■ stimulating sales
■ selling off excess material stocks

Methods of improving profits and profitability

Profits and/or **profitability** can be improved as shown in Figure 25.

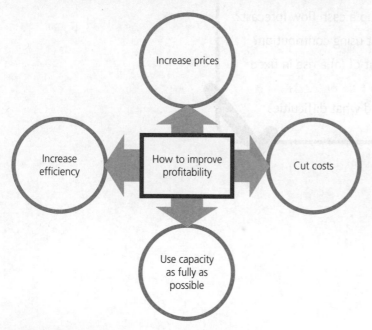

Figure 25 How to improve profitability

Difficulties improving cash flow and profit

Difficulties improving cash flow:
■ factoring: profit margin reduced and it may highlight cash flow difficulties
■ sale and leaseback: asset is removed forever and rent must now be paid

■ working capital control: customers put off by reduced credit periods and suppliers unwilling to extend credit periods

Difficulties improving profit:

■ increasing prices: reduced sales and revenue
■ cutting costs: possible reduction in quality
■ full capacity usage: problems in matching supply with demand
■ increasing efficiency: possible redundancies if technology is introduced

Do you know?

1 List three methods of improving cash flow.
2 What is meant by 'working capital'?

End of section 6 questions

1 How might it be possible for a business to have an improving gross profit margin but a falling operating profit margin?
2 How is it possible for a seemingly profitable business to fail?
3 Why is it important that a business draws up a cash flow forecast?
4 How do you calculate break-even and profit using contribution?
5 What is the effect on the break-even output of (a) a rise in fixed costs and (b) an increase in price?
6 How might a business increase its profit and what difficulties might be encountered?

7 Decision making to improve human resource performance

You need to know

- HR objectives and the value of setting them
- HR calculations
- the use of data for HR decision making and planning
- influences on job design, including Hackman and Oldham's model
- the value of changing and the influences on organisational design
- influences on delegation, centralisation and decentralisation
- how managing HR flow helps meet HR objectives
- the benefits of and how to improve employee motivation and engagement
- the value of theories of motivation
- methods of motivation and their effectiveness
- the influences on employee involvement in decision making
- managing and improving employer–employee communication and relations

7.1 Setting human resource objectives

Functions of human resources:
- manpower planning
- recruitment and selection
- training and development
- retention and employee motivation
- welfare and benefits
- dismissal and redundancy

Value of setting human resource objectives

Human resource objectives include:
- employee engagement and involvement
- talent development
- training

- diversity
- alignment of values
- number, skills and location of employees

A business that is able to fulfil these objectives is likely to benefit from:
- lower labour turnover
- higher labour retention rates
- higher productivity
- full compliance with any UK and EU labour legislation

Influences on human resource objectives

Internal and external influences on human resource objectives are shown in Table 27.

Table 27 Internal and external influences on human resource objectives

External	Internal
<ul><li>Economy</li><li>Political factors</li><li>Technology</li><li>Competitive environment</li></ul>	<ul><li>Corporate objectives</li><li>Type of product service</li><li>Style of management, including whether the HR approach is **hard** or **soft**</li></ul>

Do you know?

1 What are the various functions of the human resource department?

2 What are three internal influences on human resource objectives?

3 What are three potential benefits of a fully engaged workforce?

Key terms

Hard human resource approach Treats employees as just another asset that must be used as efficiently as possible.

Soft human resource approach Treats employees as a valuable asset with self-direction and able to be trusted.

Labour turnover The proportion of a business's staff leaving its employment.

Labour retention The proportion of employees with one or more year's service.

7.2 Analysing human resource performance

Calculating and interpreting human resource data

Labour turnover	$\dfrac{\text{number leaving during year}}{\text{average number of staff}} \times 100$
Labour retention	$\dfrac{\text{number of employees with one or more years' service}}{\text{overall workforce numbers}} \times 100$

Employees might leave a business for a number of reasons:
- low or inadequate wage levels
- poor morale and motivation
- a buoyant local labour market offering more attractive opportunities

Labour productivity	$\dfrac{\text{total output per time period}}{\text{number of employees}}$
Labour costs per unit	$\dfrac{\text{labour costs}}{\text{output}}$

Employee costs as a percentage of turnover are calculated using the formula:

$$\frac{\text{labour costs}}{\text{turnover}} \times 100$$

Monitoring employee performance may help identify business needs in terms of:
- training
- recruitment
- redundancy
- redeployment

Use of data for human resource decision making and planning

Data used in HR planning and decision making may be from internal or external sources, as shown in Table 28.

Table 28 Internal or external sources of data used in HR planning and decision making

Internal	External
■ Productivity ■ Unit labour costs ■ Retention rates ■ Labour turnover ■ Skills ■ Age profile of workers ■ Corporate objectives	■ Wage rates ■ Sales forecasts ■ Market trends ■ Competitor actions ■ Unemployment rates ■ Skills available ■ Operational capacity

Key terms

Labour productivity Measures the output per worker in a given time period and is a key measure of efficiency.

Unit labour cost A measure of the average labour cost of producing one unit of output.

Exam tip

It is important to express answers to calculations in the correct format. When calculating productivity, for example, many students express their answers as percentages and not as a number of units of output per time period.

Exam tip

It is important to look behind any labour force data that are provided. For example, two sets of productivity data may suggest that Firm A has a clear advantage. This may become less clear-cut when other factors relating to Firm B — such as quality, reliability, training etc. — are taken into account.

Exam tip

It is important to recognise that much of the data used by HR will not be from HR but will come from other functional areas such as operations and marketing.

Do you know?

1 Describe the difference between labour turnover and labour retention.
2 How do you calculate labour productivity, labour cost per unit and employee costs as a percentage of turnover?

7.3 Improving organisational design and managing the human resource flow

Structure is often depicted in an organisational chart (see Figure 26) illustrating:

- hierarchy
- chain of command
- lines of authority
- span of control

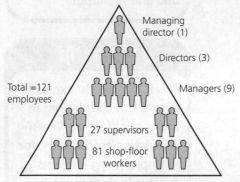

Figure 26 An organisational chart showing five levels of hierarchy

Delegation has the following benefits:
- it relieves the manager of routine tasks
- it allows the manager to focus on important issues
- it gives experience to subordinates

Influences on organisational design

Figure 27 shows the influences on organisational design.

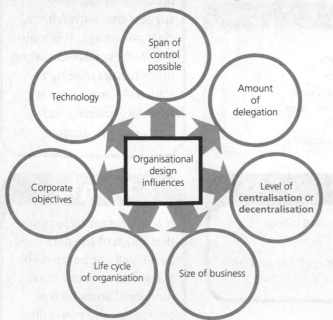

Figure 27 Organisational design influences

Influences on delegation, centralisation and decentralisation

Influences on delegation, centralisation and decentralisation include:
- uniformity of decisions
- management style
- skills and ability of workforce
- economic influences
- technology

Influences on job design

The processes and aims of job design are given in Table 29.

Table 29 Processes and aims of job design

This is the process of deciding on:	The aim being to:
contents of a job	make the job more interesting
its duties	make the job challenging
responsibilities	make the job rewarding
relationships	create a fully engaged workforce

Methods used to achieve this include:
- job rotation
- job enlargement
- job enrichment
- empowerment

The Hackman and Oldham job characteristics model (see Figure 28) addresses job design in three parts:
- core job dimensions
- critical psychological states
- personal and work outcomes

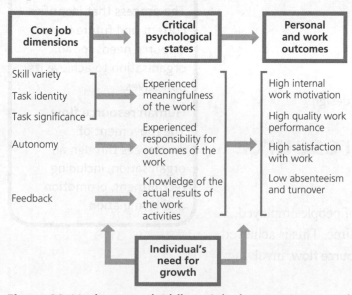

Figure 28 Hackman and Oldham job characteristics model

The goal should be to design the jobs in such a way that the core characteristics complement the psychological states of the worker, leading to positive outcomes.

The influences on job design include:

■ organisational factors   ■ behavioural factors   ■ environmental factors

Factors that affect job design are given in Table 30.

Table 30 Factors affecting job design

Organisational factors	Environmental factors	Behavioural factors
■ Task characteristics ■ Process or flow of work in organisation ■ Ergonomics ■ Work practices	■ Employee availability and ability ■ Social and cultural expectations	■ Feedback ■ Autonomy ■ Variety

Value of changing job and organisational design

Figure 29 shows the value of changing job and organisation design.

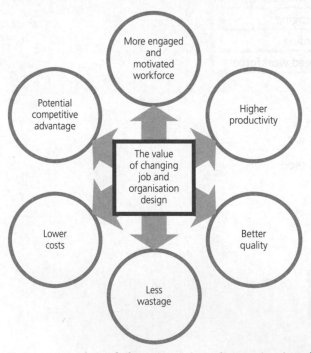

Figure 29 Value of changing job and organisation design

Managing the human resource flow

The objective of HR is to have the right number of people employed, with the right skills in the right place at the right time. This is achieved through **human resource planning** and **human resource flow**, involving:

■ recruitment and selection
■ training

- appraisal and promotion
- redundancy, redeployment and termination

Other than redundancy, an employee may be dismissed in the following circumstances:

- gross misconduct
- persistent minor misconduct
- a substantial reason

There may also be a certain amount of **natural wastage**.

> ## Do you know?
>
> 1 What are three factors that may affect organisational design?
> 2 What is meant by the term 'hierarchy'?
> 3 Why is human resource planning important?

> ## Key terms
>
> **Natural wastage** The loss of employees from a business due to retirement, resignation or death.
>
> **Motivation** The range of factors that influence people to behave in certain ways.

7.4 Improving motivation and engagement

Benefits of motivated and engaged employees

The benefits of motivated and engaged employees include:

- productivity
- recruitment and retention
- lower absenteeism
- innovation
- profitability

Value of theories of motivation

The different schools of thought and theorists of **motivation** are shown in Table 31. Maslow and Herzberg are compared in more detail in Table 32.

Table 31 Theories and theorists of motivation

Theorist	School of thought	Key features
Taylor	Scientific	■ Bethlehem Steel Company ■ Focus on the job being done and efficiency ■ Believed employees are motivated by money ■ Introduced ideas of work study and management consultancy
Elton Mayo	Human relations	■ Hawthorne studies ■ Greater focus on needs of employees ■ Type of job and level of supervision affect motivation ■ Group relationships also important

Theorist	School of thought	Key features
Maslow	Neo-human relations	■ Hierarchy of needs ■ Needs include basic, security, social, esteem and self-actualisation
Herzberg	Neo-human relations	■ Research focused on accountants and engineers ■ Factors influencing people to work divided into motivators and hygiene factors
McGregor	Neo-human relations	■ X and Y theory
Vroom	Process theory	■ Motivation depends on expectancy of outcome

Table 32 Maslow and Herzberg compared

	Maslow	Herzberg
Motivation factors (higher needs)	■ Self-actualisation needs ■ Esteem needs	■ Achievement ■ Recognition ■ Responsibility ■ Interest in work ■ Personal growth
Maintenance factors (lower needs)	■ Social needs ■ Security needs ■ Physiological needs	■ Company policy and administration ■ Supervision ■ Working conditions ■ Relationship with fellow workers ■ Salaries

How to improve employee engagement and motivation

Non-financial and financial methods can be used to improve employee engagement and motivation, as shown in Table 33 and Table 34.

Table 33 Non-financial methods to improve employee engagement and motivation

Non-financial methods	Requirements
■ Meaningful work ■ Involvement ■ Responsibility ■ Recognition	■ Right leadership style ■ Opportunity ■ Right business culture

Financial methods of motivation include:
■ piece-rate pay
■ commission
■ profit-related pay
■ performance-related pay
■ share ownership

> **Exam tip**
> You don't need to know any particular theory of motivation. However, you should know at least one theory of financial methods of motivation and one theory of non-financial methods of motivation.

> **Exam tip**
> There is not necessarily a 'right' answer as to which theory of motivation works. The success of a particular motivation technique will depend on the circumstances and the people involved.

> **Exam tip**
> The key characteristics of the non-financial methods of motivation can be directly linked to the human relations theorists and can form the basis of strong analytical arguments.

Table 34 Theories on the motivational power of financial methods to improve employee engagement and motivation

Writer	Opinions on the motivational power of pay
Frederick Taylor	Taylor saw pay as the primary motivating factor for all workers He referred to workers as 'economic animals' and supported the use of piece-rate pay
Abraham Maslow	Maslow saw pay as a reward that permitted employees to meet the lower needs on their hierarchy
Frederick Herzberg	Herzberg saw pay as a hygiene factor and a possible cause of dissatisfaction In a few circumstances pay might be a motivator if, for example, it is used as a recognition for merit

Choice of reward systems

The factors that might influence the choice and effectiveness of financial and non-financial reward systems include:

- finance
- nature of the work
- culture
- external factors

Do you know?

1 How does the scientific school of management differ from the human relations school of management?
2 List four non-financial methods of motivation.

7.5 Improving employer–employee relations

Employee involvement in decision making

The extent to which employees feel involved and appreciated may be influenced by:

- management style
- the nature of the work
- legislation

Trade unions offer employee representation and a number of benefits to members:

- they negotiate on pay and conditions of work — collective bargaining
- they discuss major changes in the workplace, such as redundancy, and help protect job security

Key term

Trade union An organised group of employees that aims to protect and enhance the economic position of its members.

- they provide a range of services, including financial and legal advice

Union membership has fallen steadily since its peak in 1979, due to:
- legislation
- the decline of traditional industries
- the increasing number of small businesses

Workers might also be represented by **work councils**:
- composed of both employee and employer representatives
- members elected to negotiate with management about working conditions, wages etc.
- nature of membership may lead to more conciliatory relationship

Employer–employee communications and relations

Good employer–employee relations lead to a more motivated and engaged workforce. This requires both:
- good communication, and
- involvement in decision making

Where disputes do happen, the help of the Advisory, Conciliation and Arbitration Service (ACAS) can be sought. Its features and services are shown in Table 35.

Table 35 Features and services of ACAS

Key features	Services
- An independent body - Set up in 1975 - Responsibility for preventing or resolving industrial disputes	- Advice - Conciliation - Arbitration

ACAS may also investigate individual cases of discrimination and has the overall aim of improving business practices to reduce the possibility of industrial disputes.

Value of good employer–employee relations

Good employer–employee relations result in:
- productivity
- employee loyalty
- better decision making

In summing up, in HR it is not just about having the right employees with the right skills; it is also about having those employees fully engaged, motivated and productive.

Do you know?

1 List three factors that may affect the level of employee involvement.

2 What do you understand to be the role of trade unions?

End of section 7 questions

1 What is the difference between a hard and soft HR approach?

2 How does a knowledge of labour turnover and market trends affect human resource planning?

3 What is delegation and why is it important to business success?

4 In what ways may changing organisational and job design help in achieving human resource objectives?

5 What are the links between the non-financial methods of motivation and the motivation theories of Maslow, Herzberg and McGregor?

6 How does ACAS help to resolve industrial disputes?

8 Analysing the strategic position of a business

You need to know

- the influences on and links between mission, corporate objectives and strategy
- the distinction between strategy and tactics, and their impact on functional decision making
- how to assess financial performance and the value of ratio analysis (SWOT internal)
- how to assess data other than financial — core competencies (SWOT internal)
- the impact of political and legal changes (SWOT external)
- the impact of economic changes (SWOT external)
- the impact of social and technological changes (SWOT external)
- the competitive environment — Porter's five forces (SWOT external)
- investment appraisal and sensitivity analysis

8.1 Mission, corporate objectives and strategy

Influences on the mission of a business

The mission of a business defines:

- what an organisation is
- why it exists
- its reason for being
- its philosophy and values (Figure 30)

The philosophy and values a business works toward:
explain its overall goals and purpose
are often a reflection of the leaders' values

 influence

size of business
activities undertaken
ownership

Figure 30 An organisation's missions, and influences on it

Exam tip

This section builds on the work covered in Year 1. It might be useful to review the section on understanding the nature and purpose of business.

There are related to the external environment in which an organisation operates, including:
- the state of the economy
- the level of competition
- government regulation

Influences on the corporate objectives and decisions

Corporate objectives are:
- the means by which a business achieves its mission
- related to the business as a whole
- SMART

Internally, corporate objectives influence:
- business ownership
- **business culture**
- business performance

External environment influences include:
- pressures of **short-termism**
- changes in the economy
- government policy
- environmental factors
- demographic trends
- competitors' actions
- technology

Distinction between strategy and tactics

The differences between **strategy** and **tactics** are illustrated in Table 36.

Table 36 Distinction between strategy and tactics

Strategy	Tactics
What we are trying to accomplish	*How* we will accomplish it
Strategies are plans	Tactics involve carrying out the plan
Medium- to long-term	Short-term
Plans formulated at top level of management	Actions formulated at middle level of management
Strategies are made for the future	Tactics are made to cope with the present

Mission, corporate objectives and strategy

The flow diagram in Figure 31 illustrates the links between the mission statement, corporate objectives and strategy.

Figure 31 The link between mission statement, corporate objectives and strategy

Once a business has set its overall mission or purpose, it is in a position to set long-term targets that will enable it to achieve or fulfil its mission. Once targets have been set, strategies or plans can be devised, aimed at meeting those targets and therefore fulfilling the mission.

Strategic decisions and functional decision making

Strategic decisions:
- relate to the business as a whole
- are taken by senior management
- are medium- to long-term in nature

Functional decision making:
- is decisions made within the functional areas of a business
- is done by functional managers themselves
- involves the action needed for that function to implement and achieve strategic decisions and targets

Value of SWOT analysis

SWOT analysis (see Figure 32) is an analytical tool, the value of which can be summed up as follows:
- helps a firm identify its core competencies, enabling it to build on its strengths
- helps a firm focus on the future given its past and present condition
- may identify opportunities that a firm can focus on to achieve maximum gains
- is a source of strategic planning as well as marketing
- helps a firm redefine and set its overall objectives

Key terms

Functional decision making Relates to the decision making within the functional areas of business: finance, marketing, operations and human resources.

SWOT analysis An analytical tool used in decision making that examines the internal strengths and weaknesses of a business as well as the external opportunities and threats.

	Strengths	Weaknesses

External

Strengths	Weaknesses
– Your specialist marketing expertise	– A lack of marketing expertise
– A new, innovative product or service	– Undifferentiated products or services
– The location of your business	(i.e. in relation to your competitors)
– Quality processes and procedures	– The location of your business
– Any other aspect of your business	– Poor quality goods or services
that adds value to your product or service	– A damaged reputation

Opportunities	Threats
– A developing market such as the internet	– A new competitor in your home market
– Mergers, joint ventures or strategic	– Price wars with competitors
alliances	– A competitor that has a new, innovative
– Moving into new market segments that	product or service
offer improved profits	– Competitors that have superior access to
– A new international market	channels of distribution
– A market vacated by an ineffective	– Taxation is introduced on your product or
competitor	service

Figure 32 SWOT analysis

Do you know?

1 What is meant by the 'philosophy and values' of a business?
2 Why may short-termism be a problem for business?
3 What is the difference between strategy and tactics?

Exam tip

In a SWOT analysis, when looking at the strengths of a business don't automatically assume a particular characteristic is a strength. For example, a loyal workforce is a strength only if it consistently performs better than a competitor's workforce.

8.2 Analysing the internal ratio analysis

How to assess the financial performance of a business

Financial performance is normally undertaken through ratio analysis, but an understanding of the balance sheet and income statement is required to do this.

Balance sheet

The **balance sheet**:

■ represents a snapshot of a business's financial position at a given time
■ shows the business's **assets**, **liabilities** and shareholders' equity

Key terms

Balance sheet A report that summarises all of an organisation's assets, liabilities and equity at a given point in time.

Assets Anything that a business owns, benefits from or has use of in generating income.

Liabilities What a business owes, the legal debts or obligations that arise during the course of business operations.

■ gets its name from the fact that the value of the assets will always be equal to the value of the money put into a business:

assets = liabilities + shareholders' equity

The structure of the balance sheet is outlined in Figure 33.

When looking at assets it is worth distinguishing between **tangible** (or physical) assets and **intangible assets**, which have no physical presence.

A number of important figures will be identified in the balance sheet.

The working capital or net current assets (see Figure 34):
■ the amount of money a business has available for day-to-day operations
■ if there is too little working capital then a business can run into cash flow problems
■ it is also important not to have too much working capital

> ## Key term
>
> **Tangible vs intangible assets** Tangible assets are actual physical assets such as land, building and machinery, whereas intangible assets are non-physical assets such as patents, copyrights and goodwill.

> ## Exam tip
>
> Reserves in the balance sheet are not held in cash but are an entry indicating past profit that has been retained in the business and spent on further non-current or fixed assets.

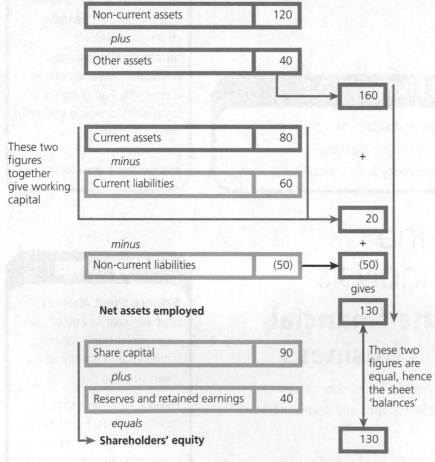

Figure 33 **Structure of the balance sheet numbers are (£m)**

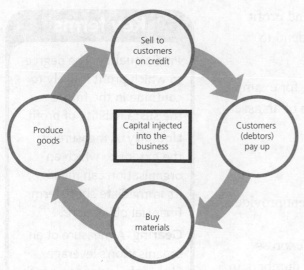

Figure 34 Working capital cycle

The following can also be determined from the balance sheet:

- the net assets or net worth of a business
- the capital employed
- the assets employed

The income statement

The **income statement** shows the income and expenditure for an accounting period and the resultant profit or (loss) made. Its structure and main elements are outlined in Figure 35.

	£m
Revenue (turnover)	250
less	
Cost of sales	190
gives	
Gross profit	60
less	
Expenses	40
gives	
Operating profit	20
plus	
Finance income	5
less	
Finance expenses	3
gives	
Profit before taxation	22
less	
Taxation	4
gives	
Profit after taxation	18

Figure 35 Structure and main elements of an income statement

Profit utilisation is decided by the board of directors and profit is either retained in the business or distributed as dividend to shareholders.

Profit quality considers the sustainability of any profit, for example whether it stems from a one-off event, such as the sale of an asset, that will not be repeated.

Ratio analysis

The information the balance sheet and income statement provide can be analysed through ratio analysis:

- ratio analysis is a tool used in financial analysis to express relationships between an organisation's accounting numbers in order to establish trends and comparisons
- the key ratios are outlined in Table 37

Table 37 Key ratios in ratio analysis

Area	Ratio	Formula
Profitability	Return on capital employed	$\dfrac{\text{net operating profit}}{\text{capital employed}} \times 100$
Liquidity	Current ratio	$\dfrac{\text{current assets}}{\text{current liabilities}}$
Gearing	Gearing ratio	$\dfrac{\text{loans}}{\text{loans + share capital}} \times 100$
Efficiency	Payable days	$\dfrac{\text{payables}}{\text{cost of sales}} \times 365$
	Receivable days	$\dfrac{\text{receivables}}{\text{revenue}} \times 365$
	Inventory turnover	$\dfrac{\text{cost of goods sold}}{\text{average inventories}}$

Value of financial ratios when assessing performance

Ratio analysis can be a valuable analytical tool provided its limitations are recognised:

- comparisons — figures need to be compared with both previous years' and those of other similar businesses to be of any use
- historical — figures are based on data from the past and may not be an indicator for the future

- **window dressing** — figures can be made to look better than they are in reality
- **limited focus** — figures focus just on financial performance and ignore other areas, for example market and technological advancement

Do you know?

1 What is the difference between gross profit, operating profit and profit for the year?
2 Why should a business not have too much or too little working capital?
3 Why is gearing useful when making a major capital investment?

8.3 Analysing the internal overall performance

For a full picture of business performance, data from other functional areas need to be analysed.

Analysing data other than financial statements

The types of data available are outlined in Table 38.

Table 38 Types of data available

Marketing	Operations	Human resources
■ Sales volume/value ■ Market share and growth ■ Market-related data ■ Competitor data ■ Consumer behaviour	■ Productivity ■ Unit costs ■ Capacity utilisation ■ Quality measures	■ Absenteeism ■ Labour turnover ■ Unit labour costs ■ Productivity

As with financial data, there is a need to compare with past years and with other similar businesses or the industry average figure.

Importance of core competencies

Core competencies are the main strengths or strategic advantages of a business. These should:
- be difficult for competitors to replicate
- provide opportunities for a business to expand
- provide significant benefits to customers

Although competencies need to be protected and developed in order to maximise an organisation's potential, there are potential downfalls:
- outsourcing to a third party, if used, has the potential to damage reputations
- things change over time, for example technology

Assessing short-term and long-term performance

In addressing performance there is a tendency to short-termism. This is most apparent in the financial measures.

There is a need to look beyond these short-term measures and consider the long-term sustainability of the business:
- this might be achieved through investment, R&D, and new products and processes
- this may lead to a temporary fall in financial performance

Value of different measures of assessing business performance

Two possible methods of measuring the wider (not just financial) performance of a business are Kaplan and Norton's balanced scorecard model and Elkington's triple bottom line.

Kaplan and Norton's balanced scorecard model

Kaplan and Norton's balanced scorecard model recommends that managers track a small number of key measures that collectively measure four dimensions, as shown in Figure 36.

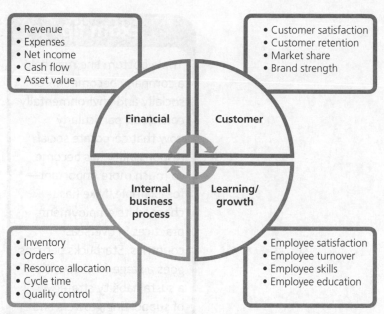

Figure 36 Kaplan and Norton's balanced scorecard model

The four dimensions need to be measured, analysed and improved together; ignoring any one dimension could result in a business losing balance and failing to thrive.

Table 39 gives the benefits and weaknesses of Kaplan and Norton's balanced scorecard model.

Table 39 Benefits and weaknesses of the balanced scorecard model

Benefits	Weaknesses
■ Provides broader view ■ May detect weaknesses early ■ May allow employees to see their importance	■ Some areas are difficult to quantify ■ Right balance between dimensions is difficult ■ Subject to compiler's bias

Elkington's triple bottom line

Elkington's **triple bottom line** emphasises the three Ps or pillars: people, planet and profit, as shown in Figure 37.

The triple bottom line was mainly intended to advance the idea of fairness and sustainability in business practice.

Although it has some merit its biggest problem is that of comparing profit, which is measured in cash terms, with people and planet, which are very difficult to quantify in the same way.

> **Key term**
>
> **Triple bottom line**
> Assesses an organisation's performance through three dimensions of performance: social, environmental and financial.

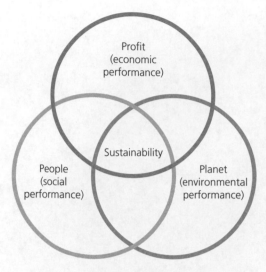

Figure 37 Elkington's triple bottom line

Do you know?

1 What is meant by the term 'core competencies'?

2 What are the two models of performance measurement?

8.4 Analysing the external environment: political and legal change

Political and legal change covers the effects of UK and EU law related to competition, the labour market and the environment. Also covered is the impact of UK and EU policy related to enterprise, the role of regulators, infrastructure, the environment and international trade.

Strategic and functional decision making

Strategic and functional decisions must be formed and undertaken within the UK and EU legal framework. This covers the areas in Table 40.

Table 40 The UK and EU legal framework

Area	Act	Detail
Competition*	Competition Act 1998	Prevents price fixing and cartels
	Enterprise Act 2002	Further strengthens Competition Act
Labour	Equality Act 2010	Brings together all acts related to discrimination
	Minimum Wage Act 1998	Introduced minimum wage
	Employment Rights Act	Sets out employee statutory rights
	Health and Safety at Work	Covers health and safety
	Working Time Regulations	Limits hours employees can legally work
	Employment Act	Covers dispute resolution, strengthens enforcement of minimum wage
	Trade Union Act	Covers closed shops, secret ballots and picketing
Environmental	Environment Protection Act	Prevents pollution from emissions
	Environment Act	Set up Environmental Agency
	Climate Change Act	Aims to make UK low-carbon economy
	Energy Act	Focuses on setting decarbonising targets

*These acts are supported and overseen by the Competition and Markets Authority.

The positives and negatives of legislation are shown in Table 41.

Table 41 Positives and negatives of legislation

Negatives	Positives
■ Increases bureaucracy and red tape ■ Can add to the costs of a business	■ Creates a level playing field ■ Makes it easier to compete

The government and EU also have an impact in the areas shown in Figure 38.

Enterprise encourages people and businesses to take initiative and be innovative by:

■ reducing red tape
■ reducing the tax burden — for example corporation tax, Patent Box
■ giving direct financial help

The aim is to create a stronger, more vibrant economy.

Key terms

Cartel Where businesses (or countries) act together as a single producer in order to influence prices, production and marketing of certain goods or services.

Discrimination Bias or prejudice resulting in the denial of opportunity or unfair treatment regarding selection, promotion or transfer of employees. It may be on grounds of age, sex, ethnic group, religion etc.

Environmental Agency A public body established in 1996 to protect and improve the environment and promote sustainable development.

Competition and Markets Authority (CMA) A non-ministerial government department responsible for strengthening business competition and preventing and reducing anti-competitive activities. (The Financial Conduct Authority is responsible for overseeing financial services.)

Enterprise In this context, refers to the willingness to take initiative in setting up or taking on a project or business venture.

Patent Box A special tax regime for intellectual property revenues that businesses have been able to elect to enter.

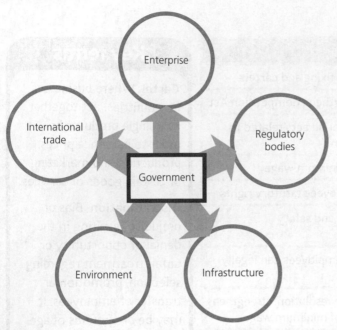

Figure 38 Impact of the government and EU

Regulatory bodies help control a wide variety of industries and professions, for example Ofwat, Ofcom and the Financial Conduct Authority.

Infrastructure is important for the smooth running of the economy and is a key determinant for inward investment.

Governments like to show a commitment to the protection of the environment, for example green belt areas around cities and subsidies for those installing renewable energy systems.

The government recognises the importance of **trading internationally** to the success of the economy and takes steps to support it, such as trade fairs or financial support for exporters.

Changes in the law and policy can have a significant impact on business in terms of costs and demand. For example, construction firms will benefit from infrastructure investment, renewable energy firms from subsidies offered, and start-up businesses and innovative firms from grants and tax incentives.

Do you know?

1 What is meant by 'anti-competitive practices'?
2 What is the meaning of the term 'discrimination' in the workplace?
3 Outline three pieces of legislation related to the environment.

Exam tips

■ Remember that legislation, although burdensome at times, does create a level playing field where all businesses are treated in the same way, leading to the effective operation of the market economy and sometimes to cost savings.

■ It is often assumed that legislation just leads to higher costs but this may not always be the case. Sometimes it can lead to cost saving: for example, environmental legislation required the introduction of filters into cement factories, which actually resulted in cost savings due to the reduction in wastage created.

Key terms

Regulatory bodies Government agencies responsible for monitoring, guiding and controlling certain industries.

Infrastructure The basic physical and organisational structures (transport, communications, utilities etc.) needed for the operation of society or enterprise.

International trade The exchange of goods and services between countries.

8.5 Analysing the external environment: economic change

This section focuses on interpretation of changes in economic data from a UK, EU and global perspective and the implications of such changes for business.

Impact of the UK and the global economic environment on decision making

Gross domestic product

Gross domestic product (GDP):

- a measure of a nation's overall economy
- an indicator of a nation's economic health
- a gauge of its standard of living
- can also be used to compare one country with another

Although the aim of governments is to achieve steady and sustained growth in GDP, this rarely happens in practice. The regular fluctuations in the level of GDP are known as the **business cycle**. This is made up of four stages, as shown in Figure 39.

Key terms

Gross domestic product (GDP) A measure of the value of all goods and services produced within a country over a specific time period, which provides a primary indicator of a country's economic health.

Business cycle or trade cycle Shows the fluctuations in economic activity, as measured by GDP, that an economy experiences over time.

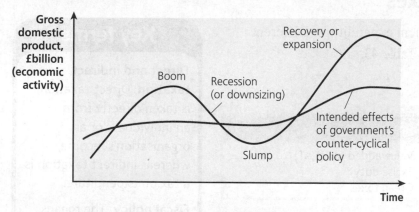

Figure 39 The four stages of the business cycle

The implications for, and responses of, business to these four stages are summarised in Table 42.

Table 42 Implications for, and responses of, business to the four stages of the business cycle

Stage of the business cycle	Possible implications for business	Possible responses of businesses to changing trading conditions
Upswing or expansion	■ Rising incomes and expenditures ■ Possible labour shortages, pushing up wages ■ Possible rise in output, encouraging expansion	■ Opportunity to charge higher prices ■ Adoption of more technology to replace expensive labour ■ Decide to invest in fixed assets ■ Operate nearer to full capacity
Boom	■ Possible rise in inflation ■ Bottlenecks in supply of materials and components ■ Unable to satisfy levels of demand as consumption rises ■ Profits likely to be high	■ Face increasing pressure to raise prices regularly ■ Seek methods to increase output (maybe producing at overseas plants) ■ Offer wage rises to avoid threat of industrial action ■ Managers plan for falling levels of demand
Recession	■ Consumers' disposable incomes start to fall ■ Demand for many products begins to fall ■ Some businesses experience financial problems ■ Excess stocks	■ Begin to emphasise price competitiveness in advertising ■ Seek new markets for existing products ■ Lay off some workers or ask them to work short time ■ Possible reduction in trade credit provided
Slump	■ Government may initiate counter-cyclical policies, e.g. lower interest rates ■ Rise in number of bankruptcies ■ Increased frequency of bad debts ■ High levels of unemployment	■ Offer basic products at bargain prices ■ Review credit control policies ■ Continue to target new markets ■ Seek to diversify product range and sell income-inelastic products ■ Reduce wage levels

Direct and indirect taxes

Taxation is required to fund government expenditure. Different direct and indirect taxes are shown in Table 43.

Table 43 Direct and indirect taxes

Direct	Indirect
■ Income tax ■ Corporation tax ■ National Insurance payments	■ Value added tax (VAT) ■ Excise duty ■ Green taxes

The ways government can use taxation and expenditure to influence the economy are known as fiscal policy:

■ increasing taxation decreases spending and slows growth
■ decreasing taxation increases spending and stimulates growth
■ government expenditure can also be used to stimulate growth

Key terms

Direct and indirect taxation Direct taxation is taken directly from an individual's or an organisation's income, whereas indirect taxation is a tax on expenditure.

Fiscal policy The means by which a government adjusts its spending levels and tax rates to monitor and influence the country's economy.

Inflation

Key features of **inflation**:
- it is the rate at which the general level of prices for goods and services is rising
- it is measured by the consumer price index (CPI)
- high inflation poses a number of problems for business, including cost pressures and reduced sales
- the government therefore seeks to provide price stability by its monetary policy, achieved through the Bank of England and the Monetary Policy Committee (MPC)
- monetary policy is the process by which the monetary authority controls money supply and interest rates in order to achieve healthy economic growth
- the MPC is a committee of the Bank of England that regulates interest rates in its attempt to maintain economic stability

Exchange rate

Changes in **exchange rate** can cause uncertainty for business and affect competitiveness, as shown in Table 44.

Table 44 Effects of changes in exchange rates

Rising exchange rates	Falling exchange rates
- Exports from the UK more expensive - Imports to UK less expensive	- Exports cheaper - Imports more expensive

Although organisations would want to trade overseas without restriction (**free trade**), they are often faced by constraints (**protectionism**), such as:
- tariffs
- quotas
- excessive rules and regulations

Protectionist policies such as these are designed to safeguard domestic industries and employment.

Reasons for greater globalisation of business

Globalisation refers to the breakdown of barriers that prevent the exchange and integration of finances, trade and ideas around the world. The reasons for greater globalisation include:
- improved transport
- technology
- more open trade
- multinational companies

Importance of globalisation for business

The impact of globalisation is both positive and negative, as shown in Table 45.

Table 45 Benefits and drawbacks of globalisation

Benefits	Drawbacks
■ Freer trade ■ Free movement of labour ■ Increased investment	■ Greater competition ■ Increased risk of takeover ■ Domestic impact of global economy ■ Tax avoidance by multinationals

> **Exam tip**
>
> The question of tax avoidance is a difficult one. The government does not want to deter direct inward investment, as companies such as Amazon and Starbucks provide a large number of jobs and the associated income tax and National Insurance contributions.

Importance of emerging economies for business

Emerging markets (e.g. BRICS) are important for a number of reasons:
■ they are large and growing markets
■ they have growing middle classes
■ they are in low-cost locations

Factors that might lead to success in emerging markets include:
■ detailed market knowledge
■ having a local partner
■ producing well-made and locally tailored products

> **Key term**
>
> **Emerging markets** Describes national economies that are progressing toward becoming more advanced through rapid growth and industrialisation.

> **Do you know?**
>
> 1 What is meant by the term 'GDP'?
> 2 How does fiscal policy differ from monetary policy?
> 3 What is meant by 'protectionism', and can you give examples of it?
> 4 Why are emerging markets important to many businesses?

8.6 Analysing the external environment: social and technological

Changes in the social and technological environment will also provide both opportunities and threats for a business.

Strategic and functional decision making

Important factors in social change are:

- demographic change
- migration
- urbanisation

Consumer tastes will also change over time, as shown in Table 46.

Table 46 Changing consumer tastes

Reasons for changing tastes	Result
Changes in fashion	More open to organic and fair trade produce
Increased awareness of alternative lifestyles	More health conscious
Rising incomes	More regular and exotic holidays
More leisure time	Eat out more often, demand more ready meals

One important aspect in all this has been the growth of **online shopping**, which has made it possible to buy almost anything from anywhere at any time.

This has impacted on the way businesses operate and created the need for an online presence involving:

- the creation of a high-quality, user-friendly website
- a carefully targeted audience
- content that is increasingly personalised
- mobile capabilities for consumers
- integrated sales channels

Technological change, of which online shopping is a part, has had a big impact on:

- the goods and services produced
- the processes to produce them
- the way in which organisations conduct their business
- the amount of information available

Table 47 gives the benefits and drawbacks of technological change.

Table 47 Benefits and drawbacks of technological change

Benefits	Drawbacks
■ Lower costs ■ Improved communication ■ Increased sales ■ Improved work environment ■ Quality	■ Pace of change ■ Competition ■ Security

Key terms

Demographic change Refers to changes in the structure of populations — age, sex etc.

Migration The movement of people between countries.

Urbanisation Refers to the increase in population living in towns and cities.

Online shopping The act of purchasing goods and services over the internet.

Technological change Relates to innovation in services provided, products produced or processes of production.

Pressures for socially responsible behaviour

Corporate social responsibility (CSR) is a significant area where greater consumer environmental awareness has led to increased pressure for CSR and CSR reporting. The reasons for and against CSR are given in Table 48.

Table 48 Reasons for and against CSR

For CSR	Against CSR
■ Cost savings ■ Brand differentiation ■ Customer and employee engagement ■ Right thing to do ■ Resources ■ Prevent government intervention	■ Impact on profit ■ Consumer perception ■ State of economy ■ The market ■ Stakeholder views

CSR has encouraged businesses to take the interests of all stakeholders into consideration during the decision-making process, rather than just those of shareholders.

This is illustrated in Carroll's **pyramid of corporate social responsibility** (see Figure 40), in which he suggested that duties to stakeholders fall under four key areas:

- economic
- legal
- ethical
- philanthropic

Key terms

Corporate social responsibility (CSR) A business approach that contributes to sustainable development by delivering economic, social and environmental benefits to all stakeholders.

Pyramid of corporate social responsibility The pyramid produced by Carroll to illustrate the four layers of corporate responsibility: economic, legal, ethical and philanthropic.

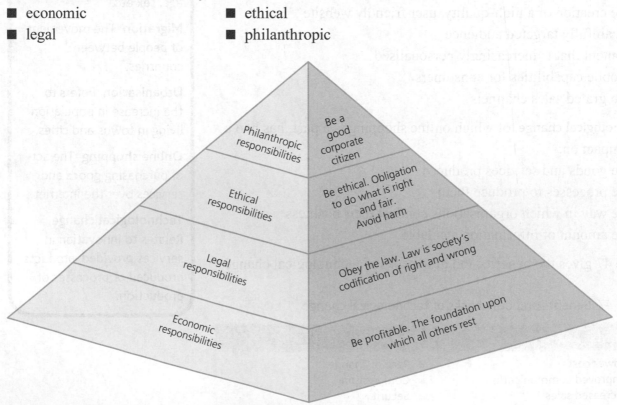

Figure 40 Carroll's pyramid of corporate social responsibility

The relevance of this pyramid perhaps lies in the framework it provides. It aids a business in understanding the necessary principles to enable social responsibility and the strategies it must develop to achieve it.

A stakeholder approach may result in increased shareholder value, as:

- employees are likely to be more engaged
- there is greater brand awareness
- consumers are perhaps more likely to buy

Although this may not always work in practice (as Primark illustrates), there are significant pressures for greater social responsibility, as shown in Figure 41.

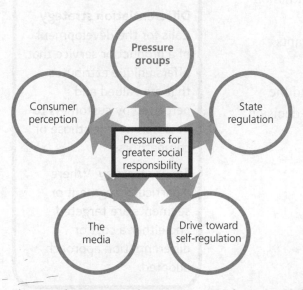

Figure 41 Pressures for greater social responsibility

Key term

Pressure group A group of people who work together in order to influence business and government decision making.

In summary, businesses should perhaps look for shareholder wealth that seeks sustainable growth and profits based on a responsible attention to a full range of stakeholder interests. In other words, they should aim to gain shareholder value while having full regard for the long-term external impact of wealth creation.

Do you know?

1 List three reasons why consumer tastes may change over time.
2 How does the stakeholder concept differ from the shareholder concept?
3 What is meant by Carroll's pyramid of corporate social responsibility and what relevance does it have for business?

8.7 Analysing the external environment: the competitive environment

The competitive environment refers to the market structure and the dynamic system in which a business competes. This is likely to impact on the flexibility of businesses that operate within it.

Porter's five forces

Porter's five forces model (see Figure 42) looks at five key areas or forces that determine competitive power in a business situation:

- competitive rivalry
- threat of substitutes
- supplier power
- buyer power
- threat of new entrants

You need to know how and why these might change, and the implications of these forces for strategic and functional decision making and profits.

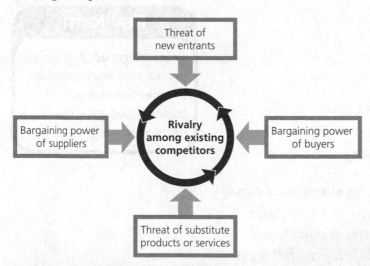

Figure 42 Porter's five forces model

As a result of analysis of the five forces, Porter identified four generic strategies that could be implemented by a business to create a competitive advantage, shown in Figure 43.

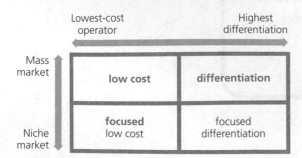

Figure 43 Porter's (generic) strategy matrix

8.8 Investment appraisal

An essential element of a successful business is that of investment, but this will involve an element of choice and risk.

Financial methods of assessing an investment

Investment appraisal helps reduce risk in investment decisions. Three methods can be identified:

1 **Payback method** is calculated using the formula:

$$\text{number of full years} + \frac{\text{amount of cost left}}{\text{revenue generated in next year}}$$

2 **Average rate of return** is calculated using the formula:

$$\frac{\text{average annual return}}{\text{initial outlay}} \times 100$$

3 **Net present value (NPV)**, or discounted cash flow, is calculated by multiplying each annual net cash flow by the appropriate **discount factor**:

- ☐ this converts future cash flows to present values
- ☐ these are then added together
- ☐ the initial investment is subtracted
- ☐ this gives a value in real terms for the return on investment
- ☐ a positive figure would indicate a worthwhile investment

Financial investment appraisal cannot eliminate risk completely as it assumes that:

- costs and revenues can be forecast accurately
- key variables such as interest rates will not change

Factors influencing investment decisions

Investment decisions are undertaken in conditions of risk and uncertainty and will be influenced by qualitative factors, such as:

- the economy
- the competitive environment
- taste and fashion
- industrial relations
- corporate image and objectives
- logistics

Key terms

Investment appraisal An analytical tool used to evaluate the attractiveness of an investment proposal.

Payback method The length of time taken to recover the initial outlay of an investment from net income.

Average rate of return Calculates the average return of an investment and expresses this as a percentage of the initial outlay.

Net present value (NPV) The current value of future income from an investment.

Discount factor The percentage rate used to calculate the present value of a future cash flow.

Exam tips

- If asked to calculate NPV in the exam, you will be supplied with the relevant discount factor to use.
- In order to avoid errors in calculating NPV it is sensible to set out your workings in a table. Not only will this help with your accuracy, it will also enable the examiner to see clearly what you are doing and easily identify any mistakes.

Value of sensitivity analysis

Sensitivity analysis is a 'what if' tool that can be used to address the problem of uncertainty, for example what if the revenues achieved from an investment were lower than expected.

Sensitivity analysis is easy to use and enables better and more informed decisions to be made.

Do you know?

1 What are the five forces in Porter's five forces model?
2 Outline three methods of investment appraisal.
3 Why does sensitivity analysis allow for a more informed decision to be made?

End of section 8 questions

1 How might a SWOT analysis help in the development of business strategies?
2 What do you understand by the term 'profit quality', and why is it important?
3 In assessing a business's financial position, name two ratios you might use and suggest on what basis you could make a judgement as to whether the business has improved its position.
4 For the functional areas of marketing, operations and human resources, draw up a table to show two performance measures of each and their formulae.
5 Outline one benefit and one drawback of Kaplan and Norton's balanced scorecard model.
6 Identify three aspects of trade union behaviour that have been targeted by trade union legislation.
7 By what means has the government encouraged enterprise?
8 Briefly explain why it is important to maintain investment in infrastructure.
9 Briefly outline how a downturn in the business cycle might affect a UK car manufacturer.
10 What would be the impact of a rise in interest rates on (a) consumers, (b) a high-geared consumer durable manufacturer, and (c) supermarkets?
11 What difficulties might a UK manufacturer face from a stronger pound?
12 Briefly account for the growth of globalisation.
13 What do you understand by corporate social responsibility (CSR) and for what reasons should businesses undertake CSR reporting?
14 How does a differentiation strategy differ from a cost leadership strategy?
15 Explain two qualitative factors that could influence an investment decision.

9 Choosing strategic direction

You need to know

- the factors influencing which markets to compete in and which products to offer
- the value of the different strategies identified by Ansoff
- the reasons for choosing and value of different options for strategic direction
- how to compete in terms of benefits and price, including the positioning models of Porter and Bowman
- the influences on the choice and value of different positioning strategies
- the benefits and difficulties of maintaining competitive advantage

9.1 Strategic direction

Strategic direction involves decisions about which markets to operate in and what products to offer. Both SWOT analysis and **Ansoff's matrix** are likely to be involved in the decision-making process.

Which markets to compete in and which products to offer?

Factors affecting choice of strategic direction include:

- objectives and attitude to risk
- cost
- barriers to entry
- competitors' actions
- ethics involved

Reasons for choosing and the value of different options for strategic direction

Ansoff's matrix identified four strategies, shown in Figure 44.

The reasons for, and value of, choosing each of Ansoff's four strategies are shown in Table 49.

Key terms

Strategic direction Refers to a course of action or plan that it is hoped will lead to the achievement of long-term goals.

Ansoff's matrix A strategic or marketing planning tool that links a business's marketing strategy with its general strategic direction.

Figure 44 Four strategies identified by Ansoff's matrix

Table 49 Reasons for and value of choosing the four strategies suggested by Ansoff

Strategy	Value
Market penetration (existing products in existing markets)	■ Quick to implement ■ Less costly ■ Market needs to have potential for growth
Product development (new product, existing market)	■ Good for businesses with strong brand name ■ Necessary in fast-changing industries ■ Useful where complementary products can be developed
Market development (existing products, new markets)	■ Good if brand name and product are already known ■ Less costly than developing new products ■ Targeted markets need to be accessible
Diversification (new product, new market)	■ Important if existing product in decline ■ Spreads risk and gives potential for growth ■ Involves greater risk

Do you know?

1 What do you understand by the term 'strategic direction'?

2 List four factors that might affect strategic direction.

9.2 Strategic positioning: choosing how to compete

Once the strategic direction has been determined it is then necessary to decide on **strategic positioning**.

Exam tip

■ Diversification is rightly described as the riskiest strategy, but don't dismiss such a strategy without studying all other information. For some businesses diversification has been hugely successful.
■ Remember that all strategies have some risk and the degree of that risk will vary according to the circumstances of the business involved. Any judgement made needs to be set in the context of the business as a whole and not just the strategy adopted.

Key term

Strategic positioning of a business Relates to how that business is perceived relative to other businesses in the same industry.

How to compete in terms of benefits and price

A business will want to position itself in such a way that it has a competitive advantage. This can be analysed in terms of two models, Porter's generic strategies and Bowman's strategic clock:

■ **Porter's generic strategies** outlines four alternative strategies (see Figure 43 on p. 90).
■ **Bowman's strategic clock** identifies eight strategic positions, shown in Figure 45.

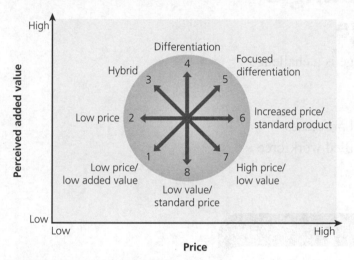

Figure 45 Bowman's strategic clock

Influences on the choice of positioning strategy

Where a business positions itself will be influenced by:
■ the business itself
■ the competition
■ the customer
■ the external environment

Value of different strategic positioning strategies

The correct positioning can provide a competitive advantage by addressing issues of:
■ price and value
■ costs
■ differentiation

This helps ensure that the strategy chosen fits:
■ clearly with the mission and objectives
■ how consumers perceive the organisation
■ consumer expectations

Benefits of having a competitive advantage

The benefits of having a competitive advantage are:
■ higher sales
■ brand loyalty
■ increased profit
■ shareholder value

Difficulties of maintaining a competitive advantage

Maintaining a sustainable competitive advantage is a challenge due to:
■ developments in technology
■ the need for investment in new products and processes
■ the need to maintain a fully engaged and skilled workforce
■ financial constraints
■ short-termism

> **Exam tip**
>
> Positioning strategies can be linked to market mapping. Identifying a particular gap in the market can lead to the correct positioning strategy being adopted.

Do you know?

1 What do you understand by the term 'strategic positioning'?
2 What is the difference between a differentiation strategy and a focus strategy as outlined by Porter's generic strategies?
3 Why are positions 6, 7 and 8 on Bowman's strategic clock unlikely to be adopted?

End of section 9 questions

1 Distinguish between market development and product development in Ansoff's matrix.
2 For what reasons might a business choose a strategy of diversification?
3 With the use of an example, explain what is meant by a low cost strategy.
4 Explain the importance to a business of having a competitive advantage.
5 Identify three reasons why it may be difficult to maintain a competitive advantage.

10 Strategic methods: how to pursue strategies

You need to know

- how and why businesses grow or retrench and the issues involved, including Greiner's model of growth
- the methods and types of growth and how to manage problems involved
- innovation, ways of becoming more innovative, its value and protection
- the reasons for targeting, operating in and trading with international markets
- the methods of entering international markets and influences on operating internationally
- Bartlett and Ghoshal's matrix
- the pressures for, impact and value of digital technology

10.1 Assessing a change in scale

Change in scale relates to the change in size of a business.

Reasons why businesses grow or retrench

Growth is important for a number of reasons:

- increased sales
- increased market share
- increased profit
- may be necessary for survival
- reduced risk
- synergy

Three further issues related to growth include:

- economies of scale
- economies of scope
- the experience curve

Key terms

Synergy The idea that the value and performance of two businesses combined will be greater than the sum of the two parts: $2 + 2 = 5$.

Economies of scale Refers to a reduction in cost as a result of an increase in size of an operating unit.

Economies of scope An economic theory stating that the average total cost of production decreases as a result of increasing the number of different products produced.

Experience curve The idea that the more you do something, the better you get at it, enabling quicker and cheaper production.

Retrenchment is the opposite of growth and means cutting down or reducing the size of a business.

Difference between organic and external growth

The differences between organic and external growth are shown in Table 50.

Table 50 Differences between organic and external growth

Organic or internal growth	External growth
■ Selling more or new products/ services ■ Targeting a wider or new market ■ Often financed by retained profit ■ Slower and less risky	■ Achieved through takeovers or mergers ■ Is growth by acquisition ■ Quicker but more risky

Managing problems of growth or retrenchment

Problems of growth are known as diseconomies of scale, and may occur due to the following:

- poor communication
- lack of control and coordination
- alienation of the workforce
- overtrading

Greiner's model of growth outlines six phases of growth and the crises associated with them, shown in Figure 46.

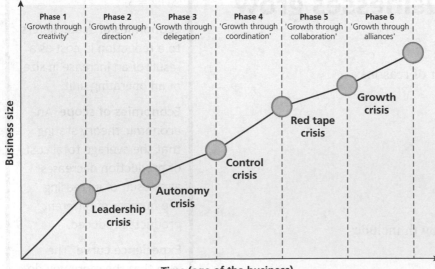

Figure 46 Greiner's model of growth

Greiner highlights the need for a scalable management model that will evolve and develop with the business and thereby perhaps help in avoiding problems of growth.

Retrenchment is the cutting down or reduction in size of a business; its characteristics are given in Table 51.

Table 51 Characteristics of retrenchment

Characteristic	Cause	Problems	Solution
Downsizing	Changes in the market		Minimise workforce impact
Sale of assets	Economic downturn	Workforce alienation	Good communication
Job losses	Failed takeover		Collaboration with trade unions

Exam tip

Sometimes a business might retrench in order to focus more closely on core competencies. Any case study material in an exam needs to be read carefully to see if this is the case.

Functional areas and growth or retrenchment

The impact of growth or retrenchment on the functional areas of business is shown in Table 52.

Table 52 Impact of growth or retrenchment on the functional areas of business

Function	Impact
Finance	Impacts on financial stability, working capital, capital investment, finance of redundancies
Marketing	Impacts on marketing mix
Operations	Impacts on unit costs, capacity, utilisation, use of technology
Human resources	Impacts on workforce planning, roles, responsibilities, organisational structure

Assessing methods and types of growth

Methods of growth include mergers and takeovers, joint ventures and franchising.

Mergers and takeovers

Mergers and takeovers are where two or more businesses agree to join together. The different types are outlined in Table 53 and shown in Figure 47.

Key terms

Mergers Where two or more businesses join together by mutual consent.

Takeovers or acquisitions Where one business acquires control over the assets of another business, either by a formal offer that is accepted (friendly takeover) or by the purchase of a controlling interest of shares (hostile takeover).

Table 53 Different types of mergers and takeovers

Type	Description	Result
Horizontal	Same stage, same production chain	Greater market presence and power
Vertical	Different stage, same production chain	Greater control over suppliers and guaranteed access to market
Conglomerate	Unrelated business	Spreads risk

Key terms

Joint venture A business arrangement where two or more businesses agree to pool their resources for the accomplishment of a specific task.

Franchising A method of growth where an existing business (the franchisor) grants another party (the franchisee) the right to use its trade name and sell its products or services.

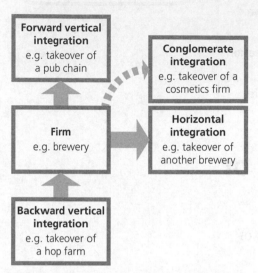

Figure 47 Types of mergers and takeovers

The failure rate of mergers and takeovers is high, due to:
■ lack of detailed research
■ resistance of employees
■ clashes of culture
■ financial pressures
■ possible lack of experience and expertise

Exam tip

A reason for undertaking a backward vertical merger is that it gives control over supplies. Sometimes, however, more control — particularly over quality and price — can be exercised when not owning the supplier, especially if a business is a major customer of the supplier.

Joint ventures

Joint ventures are where two separate organisations agree to work together for the purpose of achieving a specific task, for example to gain easier access to emerging markets.

Franchising

Franchising has a number of benefits for the franchisor:
■ relatively quick
■ finance provided by franchisee
■ franchisees are likely to be highly motivated
■ the organisation structure will be less complex

It does, however, rely on the ability and reliability of the franchise — a mistake by one franchisee could damage the brand name.

Do you know?

1 List three reasons why businesses grow.
2 What is meant by the term 'synergy'?
3 How does the experience curve differ from economies of scale?
4 What is the difference between organic and external growth?
5 List the distinguishing characteristics of horizontal, vertical and conglomerate mergers and takeovers.

10.2 Assessing innovation

An innovative business is likely to have better products and more efficient processes, and therefore is more likely to be successful.

Pressures for innovation

Innovation refers to the creation of both new products and new processes, achieved through investment in R&D.

The pressures for change through innovation include:

- survival
- shareholders
- competitive environment
- social and ethical pressures

Value of innovation

The benefits and challenges of innovation are shown in Table 54.

Table 54 Benefits and challenges of innovation

Benefits	Challenges
- Competitive advantage - Aligned to strategic positioning - Stakeholder value	- High cost - Pressures of short-termism - High failure rate in R&D

Ways of becoming an innovative organisation

The characteristics of and methods employed by innovative organisations are shown in Table 55.

Key term

Innovation The process of converting an invention into a good, service or process that creates value for a business.

Exam tip

- Don't assume that just because a business spends a large amount on R&D it will be more innovative than a business with a smaller budget. What is key is how well the budget is spent and the success rate in developing new products and processes.
- Students often confuse research and development (R&D) with market research. They are two completely separate business areas.

Table 55 Characteristics of and methods employed by innovative organisations

Characteristics	Methods employed
Culture of innovation	Kaizen
Finance available	R&D at heart of organisation
Fully engaged and talented workforce	Intrapreneurship
Acceptance of failure	Benchmarking

How to protect innovation and intellectual property

Theft of **intellectual property (IP)** is a real issue. Protection may be achieved as shown in Table 56.

Table 56 Protection available for intellectual property

Area	Protection available
Actual products	Patents
Names, logos, slogans etc.	Trademarks
Literary or musical works	Copyright

Functional areas and innovation

Innovation impacts the functional areas of a business as shown in Table 57.

Table 57 Ways innovation impacts the functional areas of a business

Function	Impact
Finance	■ Requires funding with no guarantee of a return
Marketing	■ May stem from market research or require market research to ascertain consumer reaction ■ New products or services require promotion
Operations	■ Process innovation directly affects operations ■ New products may require new processes and perhaps new capacity
Human resources	■ Fully engaged talented workforce

Do you know?

1 What is the difference between product and process innovation?

2 How does an intrapreneur differ from an entrepreneur?

3 What is meant by the term 'benchmarking'?

Key terms

Intrapreneurship The practice of entrepreneurship that exists within an established business.

Benchmarking A strategic and analytical process of continuously measuring an organisation's products, services and practices against a recognised leader.

Intellectual property Refers to creations of the mind, such as inventions, literary and artistic works, names and symbols.

Patent A government licence that gives the holder exclusive rights to a process, design or new invention.

Trademark A recognisable name, logo, slogan or design that denotes a specific product or service and legally differentiates it from others.

Copyright The legal protection provided to the work of authors, composers and artists.

Exam tip

■ As well as bringing innovation, the introduction of kaizen is likely also to lead to a more motivated and engaged workforce, leading to better overall performance.
■ Kaizen and intrapreneurship are both part of the culture of an individual business.

10.3 Assessing internationalism

Internationalism is the ideal of countries working together politically, economically and socially to achieve common goals. This has resulted in the internationalisation of business, which is the process of increasing involvement of organisations in international markets.

Reasons for operating in international markets

Reasons include:
- growth and profit
- economies of scale
- diversifying risk
- trade liberalisation
- tax

Attractiveness of international markets

Figure 48 shows the factors influencing the attractiveness of international markets.

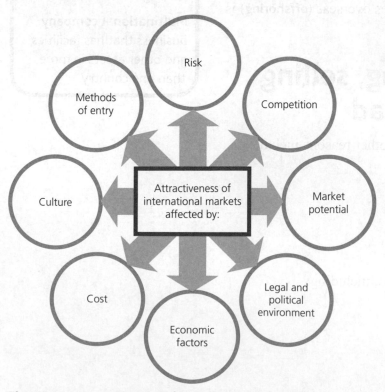

Figure 48 Attractiveness of international markets

Producing and sourcing resources abroad

Cost, quality, quantity and reliability are all major factors in the decision to produce or source resources abroad.

Entering international markets

Four main methods of entering international markets and their benefits and drawbacks are shown in Table 58.

Table 58 Four main methods of entering international markets

Method	Benefit	Drawback
Exporting	Little investment required	Possible tariffs and trade barriers
Licensing	■ Quick and low cost ■ Avoids barriers	Dependent on local producers
Alliances	Knowledge and expertise of local partner	Means sharing knowledge and technology
Direct investment	■ Direct control and avoids barriers ■ Lower costs	High risk, with potential for management and control problems

Other methods include franchising, joint ventures, and mergers and takeovers.

A business that sets up production facilities overseas (**offshoring**) is known as a **multinational company**.

Influences on buying, selling and producing abroad

Key influences are price and quality, but other reasons include:
■ skills
■ new markets
■ business-friendly framework
■ overcoming of trade barriers
■ natural resources

Producing overseas does have its problems, including:
■ ethical issues
■ control and quality
■ IP theft
■ no longer 'British' product

Key terms

Offshoring The moving of the operations of a business to another country.

Multinational company A business that has facilities and other assets in more than one country.

Managing international business

Pressures for local responsiveness relate to the tastes and preferences of the local market.

Pressures for cost reduction are likely to stem from the competitive environment.

These pressures are addressed by the **Bartlett and Ghoshal matrix** (see Figure 49), which determines four potential strategies according to pressure for local responsiveness and pressure for global integration (cost reduction).

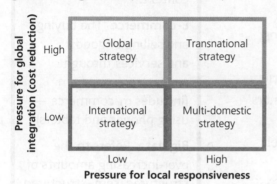

Figure 49 The Bartlett and Ghoshal matrix

Functional areas and Internationalism

The impacts of internationalism for the functional areas of business are shown in Table 59.

Table 59 Impacts of internationalism for the functional areas of business

Function	Impact
Finance	Need to finance, pressure on costs
Marketing	Researching the market, developing appropriate promotional strategies
Operations	Sourcing materials, adaptation of products, quality and capacity
Human resources	Recruitment, training and management styles

Do you know?

1 List four reasons why a business might target international markets.
2 What is meant by the term 'offshoring'?
3 What are depicted on the two axes of Bartlett and Ghoshal's matrix?

10.4 Assessing greater use of digital technology

Digital technology is increasingly becoming a pivotal part of business. No longer just a facilitator of everyday practices in business, it is now more likely to be at the heart of strategy in a business.

The pressure to adopt digital technology

Digital technologies include:

■ **e-commerce**: global reach, open 24/7 and with potential cost reductions
■ **big data**: characterised by four Vs — volume, velocity, variety and veracity; can lead to a better understanding of consumers' purchasing habits
■ **data mining**: used in market analysis, for example customer profiling, promotion
■ **enterprise resource planning**: provides improved speed, efficiency, integration and flexibility, which may result in better analysis and planning capabilities, better management of resources, and better customer satisfaction with lower costs

The pressure to introduce digital technology comes from the need:

■ for improved performance
■ to keep up with consumer and market trends

Value of digital technology

Digital technology can be used in planning and decision making, and has the benefits and drawbacks shown in Table 60.

Table 60 Benefits and drawbacks of the use of digital technology in planning and decision making

Benefits	Drawbacks
■ Reduces costs ■ Greater efficiency ■ New markets ■ Competitiveness	■ High initial costs ■ Potential for hacking ■ Dependent on reliability of systems ■ Products cannot be inspected physically

Key terms

Digital technology The term used to describe the use of digital resources to effectively find, analyse, create, communicate and use information in a digital context.

E-commerce The buying and selling of goods and services through an electronic medium (includes m-commerce — using phones and tablets).

Big data Refers to the ever-increasing amounts of structured, semi-structured and unstructured data that have the potential to be mined for information.

Data mining The process used by organisations to turn large amounts of data (big data) into useful information.

Enterprise resource planning The business management software system by which an organisation manages and integrates the important parts of its business.

Functional areas and digital technology

Digital technology impacts the functional areas as shown in Table 61.

Table 61 Impact of digital technology on the functional areas

Function	Impact
Financial	Financial analysis is quicker and easier to undertake
Marketing	Opens up new markets, enables more targeted promotions and reduces marketing costs
Operations management	Greater automation of production leading to lower costs, better quality, greater flexibility and reduced waste
Human resources	More flexible, multiskilled workforces operating under better conditions

Do you know?

1 What is meant by the term 'digital technology'?
2 What is the difference between the terms 'big data' and 'data mining'?

End of section 10 questions

1 Briefly explain why a business might undertake a strategy of retrenchment.
2 With the use of an example, describe what is meant by 'economies of scope'.
3 Describe briefly Greiner's model of growth.
4 Identify three reasons why a business might undertake franchising as a form of growth.
5 What is meant by the term 'intellectual property' and how might it be protected?
6 Why might a business decide to re-shore production back to the UK?
7 What is enterprise resource planning and what benefits does it bring?
8 Briefly outline two possible problems associated with introducing greater digital technology.

11 Managing strategic change

Strategic change can be defined as a restructuring of an organisation's business or marketing plan that is typically performed to achieve an important objective. It is therefore a change in the fundamental strategy of an organisation, which is likely to create issues of identity, culture, direction etc. that will need careful management.

11.1 Managing change

Change needs to be managed in a structured way in order to meet organisational goals, objectives and mission.

Causes of and pressures for change

Pressures for change may be external or internal, as shown in Table 62.

Table 62 External and internal pressures for change

External	Internal
■ Changing consumer tastes and fashion ■ Political changes ■ Government action ■ Economic changes ■ Competition ■ Technological changes	■ Employee attitudes ■ Leadership change ■ Restructuring

Change may also be either **incremental** over a number of years or one-off **disruptive** change.

Change within business is inevitable and the management of change will be a key factor in the success of a business. **Lewin's force field analysis** can help in managing change by examining the forces for change (driving forces) and against it (restraining forces). This is illustrated in Figure 50.

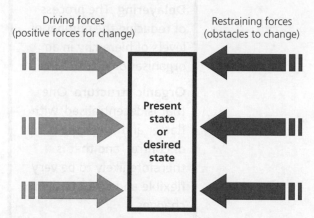

Figure 50 Lewin's force field analysis

Although these forces work in opposite directions there normally exists a balance or equilibrium within a business. For a change to occur the driving forces would need to be greater than the restraining forces, thus changing the balance or equilibrium.

Force field analysis (FFA) investigates that balance of power, identifying the most important players (stakeholders) and target groups and how to influence them. In conducting an FFA the following steps might be taken:
- identify the current situation
- identify the desired situation
- list all the driving forces
- list all the restraining forces
- evaluate each of the driving forces and restraining forces, giving each a value on a 1–10 scale where 1 is very weak and 10 extremely strong
- if change is viable, develop a strategy to strengthen the key driving forces and weaken the key restraining forces

The value of change

At a basic level if something isn't working then it needs to be changed but, in addition, this change should be seen as a good thing as it will move an organisation forward and without it stagnation is likely to result. In today's fast-moving environment change should therefore be embraced by business. The value of change can be summed up in the following factors:

- greater flexibility
- enables progress
- provides opportunities
- satisfies customer needs
- challenges the current situation

The value of a flexible organisation

A flexible organisation will benefit from:

- greater competitiveness
- improved efficiency
- teambuilding

Flexibility may be demonstrated in:

- **restructuring**
- **delayering**
- flexible employment contracts
- **organic** rather than **mechanistic structures**

The value of managing information and knowledge

Information management focuses on retrieving, organising and analysing data and information and as such creates useful knowledge.

Knowledge management focuses on knowledge, understanding and wisdom and is the process of making effective decisions and taking effective actions.

Managing information correctly leads to increased knowledge, resulting in the creation and implementation of plans and strategies that are more likely to improve performance.

Barriers to change and how to overcome them

Change is inevitable and essential for the long-term progress and even the survival of an organisation.

> ## Key terms
>
> **Restructuring** Involves a fundamental internal organisational change that alters the roles and relationships of those involved.
>
> **Delayering** The process of reducing the number of levels of hierarchy in an organisational structure.
>
> **Organic structure** One that is decentralised, with flatter and wider spans of control, and that is therefore likely to be very flexible and adapt easily to changes.
>
> **Mechanistic structure** One that is hierarchical and bureaucratic, with centralised authority and formal procedures and practices.

Barriers to change include:

- employee resistance
- management behaviour
- inadequate resources
- organisational culture

J. P. Kotter and L. A. Schlesinger identified four key reasons for employee resistance and six ways to overcome this, shown in Table 63.

Table 63 Kotter and Schlesinger's reasons for employee resistance and ways to overcome them

Reasons for resistance	Ways to overcome
<ul><li>Parochial self-interest</li><li>Misunderstanding and lack of trust</li><li>Different assessments</li><li>Low tolerance of change</li></ul>	<ul><li>Education and communication</li><li>Facilitation and support</li><li>Participation and involvement</li><li>Participation and involvement</li><li>Negotiation and bargaining</li><li>Explicit and implicit coercion</li></ul>

Do you know?

1 What is the difference between incremental and disruptive change?
2 What is the value of change for a business?
3 What is meant by the term 'restructuring'?
4 What is the difference between mechanistic and organic structures?
5 List four barriers to change.

11.2 Managing organisational culture

Organisational culture is often defined as 'the way we do things around here'.

Importance of organisational culture

Culture determines how employees interact and is important for a number of reasons:

- organisational identity
- direction
- loyalty of workforce
- healthy competition among workforce
- attitude to change

Key term

Organisational culture
A system of shared assumptions, values and beliefs that govern how a business operates.

The culture adopted can vary. It might be:

■ bureaucratic: governed by formal rules and operating systems
■ entrepreneurial: characterised by a high level of risk and creativity

Handy described four types of culture (see Figure 51):

■ power culture
■ role culture

■ task culture
■ person culture

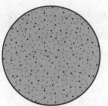
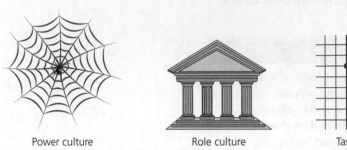

| Power culture | Role culture | Task culture | Person culture |

Figure 51 Handy's cultural model

Geert Hofstede identified six dimensions of national culture that distinguish countries rather than individuals (see Figure 52).

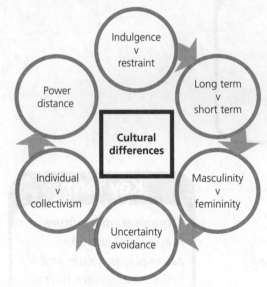

Figure 52 Hofstede's national cultures

Influences on organisational culture

The influences on organisational culture include:

■ age of business
■ size of business
■ leadership style
■ objectives of organisation
■ nature of business
■ employees

Changing organisational culture

Although organisations and culture will evolve over time, there are a number of specific reasons or circumstances that are likely to lead to a culture change, shown in Table 64.

Table 64 Reasons for culture change and problems with change

Reason	Problem
■ Toxic culture ■ Change of leader ■ Change of ownership ■ Changing market conditions	■ Resistance to change ■ Scale of change ■ Cost

Do you know?

1 What is meant by the term 'organisational culture'?
2 What is the difference between Handy's power and role cultures?
3 List four reasons for changing culture.

11.3 Managing strategic implementation

Strategic implementation is critical to success as it addresses the who, where, when and how of reaching the desired goals and objectives.

How to implement strategy effectively

The following may help in successful strategy implementation:
■ a clear understanding of the circumstances
■ the commitment of management and workforce
■ the willingness to change
■ the ability to monitor and measure progress
■ strong leadership
■ good communication

Key term

Strategic implementation Refers to the activities used within business to manage the execution of a strategic plan.

Leadership and communications in strategic implementation

Leadership is crucial. For efficient implementation the leader must:
- be committed
- be able to communicate effectively
- monitor progress
- make any necessary changes

Good communication is also essential:
- key stakeholders need to be identified
- channels and timings must be determined
- this leads to greater enthusiasm and commitment to the strategy

Organisational structure and strategic implementation

There is no one optimal organisation structure for a given strategy, but the structure is likely to evolve and develop with the business.

Sometimes strategy implementation may require a redesign of organisational structure in order to make it relevant to the strategy.

Possible structures include:
- **functional**
- **product-based**
- **regional or geographic**
- **matrix**

Value of network analysis in strategic implementation

A useful tool in strategic implementation is **network analysis** (or **critical path analysis**).

The network diagram itself will consists of two elements (see Figure 53):
- activities — shown by arrows and identified by a letter
- nodes — shown as circles and numbered

Key terms

Functional structure Where business is organised into smaller groups based on functional areas: marketing, finance, operations etc.

Product-based structure Based upon the product or a product line, where all functions related to that product are delegated.

Regional or geographic structure Where a business has separate structures dependent on a region or geographical area.

Matrix structure Where the structure is based around a major project or task, and specialists from the various functional areas are assigned to the project.

Network analysis A method of planning a project in order to identify the most efficient way of completing it.

Critical path analysis A method of planning a project in order to identify the most efficient or quickest way of doing it, i.e. the critical path.

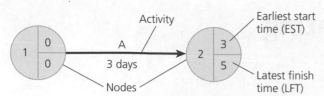

Figure 53 Activities and nodes in network diagrams

It shows the following:

- the sequence in which activities should be undertaken
- the length of time taken by each activity
- the earliest start time at which each activity can commence
- the latest finish time at which each activity must be completed to avoid delaying other activities

The diagram can be used to calculate float or spare time using the formula:

$$LFT - duration\ of\ activity - EST$$

It also shows the **critical path**.

The benefits and drawbacks of network analysis are shown in Table 65.

Table 65 Benefits and drawbacks of network analysis

Benefits	Drawbacks
<ul><li>Encourages planning, which helps reduce the risk of delays and other problems</li><li>More efficient use of resources</li><li>Time and money can be saved by operating activities simultaneously</li><li>Enables better problem solving</li></ul>	<ul><li>Dependent on accuracy of information used</li><li>Difficult to represent complex activities</li><li>Can be affected by changing external factors</li></ul>

Do you know?

1 Why are leadership and communication so important to successful strategy implementation?

2 What are the differences between functional, product-based and matrix organisational structures?

11.4 Problems with strategy and why strategies fail

Although successful implementation of a well-planned strategy can give an organisation a competitive advantage, the failure rates have been estimated at anywhere between 60% and 90% by various studies.

Key term

Critical path The sequence of activities that must be completed on time if the whole project is not to be delayed. It is indicated by two small dashes across the relevant activities.

Exam tips

- There is often a temptation with network diagrams to focus on the calculation of ESTs and LFTs and so on, while ignoring the benefits and drawbacks of network analysis. A focus on the pros and cons will help you write both analytically and evaluatively.
- Although you should make sure you can draw a network from scratch and be prepared to draw one as this helps your understanding, you are more likely in an exam to be asked to amend a network or calculate ESTs, LFTs or the float.

Difficulties of implementing strategy

Difficulties include:

- goals may not be fully understood by the workforce
- targets may not be clear
- employee capabilities
- key personnel leaving
- a lack of direction and commitment
- unforeseen events
- keeping to deadlines

Planned vs emergent strategy

The differences between **planned** and **emergent strategy** are shown in Table 66.

Table 66 Differences between planned and emergent strategy

Planned strategy	Emergent strategy
- Assumes a smooth change - Little disruption - Involves laying down timetables - Ignores the dynamic environment - Does not address the continuous need for structural adaptation	- Develops over time - Can be disruptive - Part of every manager's role - Characterised by unforeseen events

Reasons for strategic drift

Strategic drift usually occurs when organisations are unable to keep pace with changes in their external environment.

Although it may be easy to see major changes with hindsight, it is not so easy to see them when they are actually happening. Possible causes include:

- the technological environment
- lagged performance
- the culture
- a lack of monitoring

The strategic plan therefore needs a degree of flexibility and manoeuvrability to adapt to the changing situation.

Four phases of strategic drift have been identified and are illustrated in Figure 54.

Key terms

Planned strategy One that managers intend to implement, using a carefully laid plan to achieve the desired position.

Emergent strategy An unplanned strategy that develops over time and is based on the belief that change is not a series of linear events.

Strategic drift Occurs when a business responds too slowly to changes in its external environment, resulting in the strategic plan no longer being appropriate.

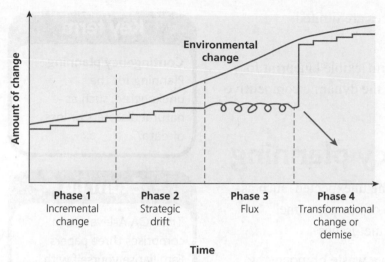

Figure 54 Strategic drift

Divorce between ownership and control

As a business grows and converts to a plc, a **divorce of ownership and control** may develop. As a result:

- owners may no longer have control
- conflicts of interest may develop:
  - ☐ shareholders want profit maximisations
  - ☐ directors want long-term growth

As a result, a system of **corporate governance** exists, which involves:

- accountability
- fairness
- transparency
- responsibility

Evaluating strategic performance

Strategy evaluation might be undertaken in the following ways:

- reviewing the underlying factors in an organisation's strategy
- comparing expected results with actual results (measuring performance)
- analysing any variances in performance
- identifying corrective actions to ensure performance conforms with the strategy

Value of strategic planning

Strategic plans can help create value as they:

- give purposeful direction to the organisation and outline measurable goals
- may identify and help build a competitive advantage

- assist in making choices where resources are limited
- can save time as clear priorities are set

A strategic plan should not be seen as an inflexible blueprint for the future as it may need to evolve due to the dynamic competitive environment.

Value of contingency planning

Contingency planning can help deal with the unexpected, such as:
- natural disasters
- loss of data
- loss of key personnel
- product issues

Although contingency planning is seen as a waste of money by some, it can provide damage limitation by:
- enabling a quicker response
- being likely to save money
- providing customer reassurance

Do you know?

1 What is the difference between planned and emergent strategy?

2 What is meant by the term 'divorce of ownership and control'?

3 What is the importance of strategic planning and evaluation?

4 What is the meaning of the term 'contingency planning'?

End of section 11 questions

1 In Lewin's force field analysis, what must happen to the balance of driving and restraining forces for change to occur?

2 Identify three different flexible employment contracts and briefly explain the importance to a business of flexible contracts.

3 Explain the link between knowledge and information management.

4 List the six ways of overcoming resistance to change given by Kotter and Schlesinger.

5 List the six dimensions of Hofstede's national cultures.

6 Explain two influences on organisational culture.

7 Briefly explain two factors that are likely to lead to successful strategy implementation.

8 Outline how network analysis can help in successful strategic implementation.

9 Define what is meant by 'strategic drift' and briefly explain two reasons for it.

10 Why is good corporate governance important in a market economy?

Key term

Contingency planning Planning for the unexpected, such as natural disasters or loss of data.

Exam tip

The AQA A-level exam comprises three papers. Familiarise yourself with these papers and the skills required for answering them so that you know what to expect and the amount of time to allocate to each question. In Paper 1, for instance, the last question is worth 25% of the marks and is an essay. It is important you have enough time to answer this question properly. **Get your timing right.**

Remember that all three papers address the *whole* specification covered in Years 1 and 2, so you must be prepared to draw on the whole of that knowledge in planning and writing your answers. **Read questions carefully** to identify the focus and don't forget to **plan**.